FEMININE IN THE CHURCH

FEMININE IN THE CHURCH

Edited by Monica Furlong

First printed in Great Britain 1984
SPCK
Holy Trinity Church
Marylebone Road
London NW1 4DU

British Library Cataloguing in Publication Data

Feminine in the Church.
   1. Ordination of women—Catholic Church
  I. Furlong, Monica
  262'.142'088042   BV676
  ISBN 0-281-04120-2

Photoset and printed in Great Britain by
Photobooks (Bristol) Ltd.

To the
Society for the Ministry of Women in the Church,
the Anglican Group for the Ordination of Women,
and Christian Parity, the ancestors,
with love and gratitude.

Contents

Contents

The Contributors

John Austin Baker has been the Bishop of Salisbury since 1982, and from 1980-82 was Chairman of the Church of England Board for Social Responsibility Working Party on Nuclear Weapons which produced the report *The Church and the Bomb*. He is currently a member of the World Council of Churches' Standing Commission of Faith and Order, and has published four books.

George Carey has been on the staff of three theological colleges: Oakhill College, London, St John's College, Nottingham, and now Trinity College, Bristol. Prior to his present appointment he was Vicar of St Nicholas' Church, Durham.

Peter Clark was brought up in Aberdeen, working first as a professional actor before taking orders. He is now assistant curate in the inner-city area of Chapeltown, Leeds.

Eric Doyle entered the Franciscan Order (Friars Minor) in 1954 and was ordained priest in 1961. He teaches theology and church history in the House of Studies of the English Province of Friars Minor. He has published articles in various periodicals on theology and spirituality, and is a frequent broadcaster.

Monica Furlong has worked as a journalist and BBC producer. She now spends most of her time on novels and biography, and she is the biographer of Thomas Merton. She has two grown-up children and is the Moderator of the Movement for the Ordination of Women.

Anne Hoad is a mother of two young children and is married to a doctor. Made a deaconess in the Deaconess Community of St Andrew, she has now been a deacon for fifteen years and has worked as a student chaplain and as a lay training officer. She is now attached to St Luke's, Charlton, London.

Janet Morley is an Anglican who worships regularly with Methodists as her husband is a Methodist minister. She has three children and has taught language, literature, creative writing and women's studies. She belongs to the Christian Feminist movement. She is secretary to a working group of the BCC on the Community of Women and Men in the Church.

Richard A. Norris, Jr, is at present Professor of Church History in the Union Theological Seminary, New York, and a priest of the Diocese of New York.

Jill Robson was born into the Church of England but converted to Roman Catholicism at the age of 21. She married an engineer and had three children, then studied psychology and philosophy as a mature student and obtained a PH D. She is now Senior Tutor on the East Midlands Ministry Training Course in Nottingham.

Henriette Santer was born and brought up in the Netherlands. She is married to Mark Santer, Bishop of Kensington, and has three children. She is a clinical psychologist working in the National Health Service.

Mary Tanner has taught Old Testament at Hull and Bristol Universities and was then on the staff of Westcott House, Cambridge. She has also been involved in the WCC's study on the Community of Women and Men in the Church.

Rowan Williams has been on the staff of Westcott House, Cambridge, worked in a council estate parish in Cambridge, and is now a university lecturer in early Christian thought at the University of Cambridge. He has travelled, taught and learned in India, Africa and the USA, and is married to Jane Williams.

Jane Williams read theology at Cambridge, where she met and married Rowan Williams. Her interest in the feminist movement started early and her belief that women should be ordained has something to do with the fact that the male priests in her family have helped her to believe that women, too, are made in God's image.

Introduction

These essays are part of a lively debate in the Church of England
– a debate of which the narrow end, as it were, is the ordination
of women to the priesthood, and the broad end is the full
evaluation of women within the Christian community, and
maybe within society as a whole. It is a large subject and we are
not rash enough to imagine we can cover it adequately or
comprehensively. A few aspects of it are well-worn and have
more to do with attempts to counter misogynistic arguments
than with genuine attempts at new thinking. But we have tried,
both here and elsewhere, not to cramp ourselves into defensive
postures, but to work freshly with new ideas. Obviously in an
institution with deep historic roots like the Christian Church
this means a constant and grateful awareness of the nourishment of the past, although for women, as for some others
within the Church, it cannot mean an uncritical or blind
acceptance of attitudes which have been wounding and
deforming. For both women and men the debate takes courage,
wisdom, hope that things can be different, charity towards
opponents and, above all, a readiness to recognize our fear of
change.

Two attitudes to women emerge very clearly from a study of
the history of the Church. One is that woman is Eve, the
temptress, the one who disturbs man, leads him away from his
spiritual preoccupations and is for him the incarnation of
sensuality; the Church Fathers repeatedly discussed women in
these sort of terms. The other attitude, which revolved around
the cult of the Virgin Mary, was one which put woman on a
pedestal, as a 'pure' being, far above man's sensual state;
woman as mother, and therefore a being who was sexually
taboo. Nowadays it is difficult not to see the first attitude as an
example of 'projection' on the part of men; uncomfortable with

1

the disturbing aspects of sexual desire, and not knowing how to integrate spiritual and sensual aspects of himself, man puts the blame on woman. 'The woman tempted me and I did eat.' In a sense this gives woman too much power, a power which must be countered by dominating and exploiting her. It also makes sexuality a continuing, unhappy embarrassment within the Christian religion. The second attitude, that of putting woman on a pedestal, is a harder one for women to resist or see through, until they perceive that this gross romanticization of them, the flight from recognition of their sexuality, often conceals a profound hostility towards them on the part of men. What it does not permit is any recognition of woman as she really is, a human being with both sensual and spiritual needs.

That both of these attitudes have served to keep women out of the priesthood is naively and rather amusingly evident in the report of the Archbishops' Commission on Women and the Ministry of 1936:

> We maintain that the ministration of women will tend to produce a lowering of the spiritual tone of Christian worship, such as is not produced by the ministrations of men before congregations largely or exclusively female. It is a tribute to the quality of Christian womanhood that it is possible to make this statement; but it would appear to be a simple matter of fact that in the thoughts and desires of that sex the natural is more easily made subordinate to the supernatural, the carnal to the spiritual, than is the case with men; and that the ministrations of a male priesthood do not normally arouse that side of female nature which should be quiescent during the times of the adoration of almighty God. We believe, on the other hand, that it would be impossible for the male members of the average Anglican congregation to be present at a service at which a woman ministered without becoming unduly conscious of her sex.

The blend of flattery, archness and rejection is one which many women will recognize and flinch at; any minute, it seems, the writer will propose a toast to 'the Ladies: God bless 'em'.

This coy approach to the subject was to be blasted away within a decade. In 1944 Bishop R.O. Hall ordained Deaconess Li Tim Oi priest at Xing-Xing in the Hong Kong diocese. Florence Li Tim Oi served a mixed Chinese and European congregation on the Japanese-occupied island of Macao. Because no priest was available and the congregation was in dire need, Bishop Hall summoned Li Tim Oi through the Japanese lines into free Hong Kong and ordained her. At some considerable personal risk she made the journey there and back, an act which came to symbolize the courage with which women have since sought ordination in the face of formidable opposition. The news leaked slowly back to Britain and the ordination was condemned as 'a mistake' by the *Church Times*. Li Tim Oi was soon forced to relinquish her orders because of the enormous pressure on Bishop Hall, and the Lambeth Conference of 1948 declared that women's orders were against Anglican tradition and 'would gravely affect the internal and external relations of the Anglican Communion'.

Ten years later Lambeth was obviously beginning to feel uncasy about its intransigence. It commented on how well trained women church workers were, exhorted churches to make better use of them, and suggested, with unconscious irony, that they might come in useful where 'pioneer work has to be done'.

In 1968 the Conference began to make a new sound. 'The Conference affirms its opinion that the theological arguments as at present presented for and against the ordination of women are inconclusive.' This was reluctant enough; short of outright refusal to ordain women diffidence could scarcely be more marked, but it was the first stone tumbling down the mountainside. The mountain had begun to move.

Events happened quickly. The Anglican Consultative Council, meeting at Limuru, Kenya, in 1971, passed the controversial Resolution 28. This encouraged debate of women's ordination throughout Anglican churches, and permitted bishops to ordain women with the approval of their Provinces.

The new Bishop of Hong Kong, Bishop Baker, at once ordained two women, and Li Tim Oi resumed her orders.

The ordination of women had previously been a subject which aroused limited interest in the Church; suddenly debate and action intensified. In the United States women moved forward quickly seeking ordination. The Episcopal Church of the USA had shown itself split, with the House of Bishops voting in favour and the House of Deputies of the General Convention voting against. Confronted with this position of deadlock, eleven women sought the co-operation of sympathetic bishops and were irregularly ordained at Philadelphia in 1974.

In 1975 the General Synod of the Anglican Church of Canada voted substantially for the ordination of women and in the same year the General Synod of the Church of England voted in favour of the motion 'That this Synod considers that there are no fundamental objections to the ordination of women to the priesthood'. However, they rejected a motion to 'remove the legal and other barriers'.

Within the next few years women were legally ordained in the Churches of New Zealand, the United States and Canada, and in Britain the hopes of many women who wished to be ordained were raised; it seemed more than likely that the Church of England would follow the example of other churches. The shock on 8 November 1978, therefore, when the Synod voted against removal of legal barriers, was very severe. 'We asked you for bread and you gave us a stone', Una Kroll shouted from the gallery when the result was announced; like many who had worked for women's ordination she felt a sense of betrayal. The pain of this rejection of women was to have extensive repercussions.

A number of small organizations had already been working for many years trying to raise Christian consciousness on ordination, and other related issues. The ecumenical body, the Society for the Ministry of Women in the Church (founded in 1929), the Anglican Group for the Ordination of Women and the Christian Parity Group (the most radical, concerned with relations between women and men) had all played their part; Mollie Batten, Margaret Roxburgh, Rachel Moss, Christian Howard, Diana McClatchey, Edith Fyleman, Pauline Webb (a Methodist), Una Kroll and Elsie Baker had significantly shaped their policies.

As a result of the disappointment of 1978 members of these groups and others met to form the Movement for the Ordination of Women (MOW). A working party - Canon

4

Trevor Beeson, Diana Collins, Margaret Webster, Kathleen Burn and Christian Howard – prepared a constitution and, at a big meeting in July 1979 held during Synod week so that bishops and Synod members could more easily attend, MOW was launched. Soon it had its own office, at Napier Hall in Westminster, and an executive secretary, Margaret Webster.

Right from the beginning it represented a wide range of views and varieties of churchmanship from the most radical to the most conservative and orthodox. There were some quite severe disagreements on policy which were faithfully and honestly argued out. Members of MOW frequently reminded themselves and each other that they were working on a new model of what a Christian community might be, a model dedicated to openness, listening, expression of anger where it seemed necessary, consultation, informality, and consideration of the needs and wishes of women. Active both nationally and in local groups, MOW found itself, somewhat to its own surprise, slowly and steadily becoming an influence in the Church, as its numbers soared beyond the usual membership of Church organizations. It was clear that it was tapping a new source of energy, that it had a dynamism not often seen in the Church of England.

From the first it had eschewed fanaticism and extremism. Its task, as it saw it, was to bring about change in the Church, by dialogue, discussion, theological argument, education in all its forms, as well as by working for canonical change. Both in MOW and in some of the overlapping Christian feminist groups there was an upsurge of interest in liturgical language, in theology, in the relation of feminist insights to Christian history, and of Christian history to feminist insights. Groups, conferences, papers, dialogues, experimental liturgies, house meetings, abounded. There were exhibitions and entertainments, articles and television appearances, acts of witness at ordinations. Suddenly there was a ferment of ideas.

Inevitably such an organization encountered formidable opposition, hostility and even harassment. Some of it came from Anglo-Catholics using the argument 'from tradition'; two thousand years of not ordaining women made it impossible to begin now, they claimed. Another whole area of debate concerned the idea of the priest at the altar as the 'icon' of

Christ; since women differ genitally from men (so runs this argument), they cannot 'represent' him. Some Evangelicals base their opposition on St Paul's strictures about women 'keeping silence' in the churches, and on his words about man being 'the head' of the woman. Upon such teaching a whole edifice about the 'subordination' of women and the 'domination' of men was constructed.

Rather less serious opposition figured in the *Church Times*, whose correspondence columns are a rich, and seemingly inexhaustible, mine of misogyny. One cleric had the exciting fantasy that if women were ordained we should have a race of lascivious 'priestesses' similar to those in first-century cults. Another thought it was no good ordaining women 'because they still gaze pathetically towards the male when the car won't go'. The daddy of them all was Francis Bown of Ecclesia uttering his resounding crow of victory after the Synod vote in 1978: 'The cause of women priests is defeated for the foreseeable future, and the pressure to resurrect the issue which can be expected from a few militant and hysterical feminists must be firmly resisted.'

As time went on the arguments underwent a sea-change. We began to hear not so much that the idea was wrong as that it was not 'expedient'. The time was 'not ripe'. We were 'divisive' even to bring the painful subject up at all, and fathers in God used to ask us, more in sorrow than in anger, how we could be so tactless, so thoughtless, so *selfish*, as to disturb everyone so unnecessarily. The ordination of women would 'come one day', provided we took no action to hasten it. Any action on our part would be 'counter-productive'. In the words of Ogden Nash: 'People who have what they want are very fond of telling people who haven't what they want that they really don't want it.'

It was also pointed out that the rise of ecumenism had made the goal of the ordination of women more remote. Neither the Roman Catholic Church nor the Orthodox Church was noted for an enlightened attitude to women, but 'unity' with them was seen as a more desirable and urgent goal than revising our own theory and practice about the ministry of women.

Underlying many 'intellectual' arguments against women's ordination there often seemed to be fearful and primitive attitudes peeping out. Although no one argued any more as ingenuously as the Archbishops' Commission of 1936 had done, sophistication often hid doubts about women which retained their ancient power but which were hard either to articulate or to respond to in rational ways. Thus, women were a source of temptation and disturbance and must be kept out of the 'holy places'. Women were 'aggressive', and given half a chance, would start dominating men. Women, particularly pregnant or menstruating women, were in some way 'unclean', a taboo found in Judaism and echoed to this day in some Greek Orthodox practices. Such arguments are in some sense unanswerable since, like racial prejudice, they are based on primitive emotion not easily accessible to the rational mind.

No amount of fear, however, could stem the rapid change that was occurring throughout the Anglican Communion. Between 1974 and 1983, six provinces out of sixteen began to ordain women; there are now approaching 700 women priests. Many British women and men visiting the United States and Canada began to experience the ministry of women as celebrants and preachers, and they found that they were moved and delighted by the experience, that it seemed entirely natural and congenial *once you had seen it happen*. Women in churches here began to take an active part in liturgy - reading, preaching, serving, administering, interceding. Visiting women priests became friendly with groups in this country, ministering to those who specially wished to be served by a woman priest. A strong friendship began to be forged between women all over the Anglican Communion, an international network of help and encouragement between women who had achieved ordination and others in churches which still denied it. Some British women, unwilling to wait for the snail-like canonical processes of change in this country, went overseas to train for and seek ordination, and several have now taken up ministry in the United States and Canada.

It is against this background that we are publishing this book. Soon the Synod will again be debating the ordination of women and since we believe that the issue has implications for

Church and society which go beyond itself, we are concerned that the matter should be thought about deeply by Synod members and others. We wish to encourage an atmosphere of sensitive, loving, and thoughtful debate, debate which recognizes that we are talking of offering new life, energy and hope to the Church.

The essays cover a wide spectrum of argument. George Carey addresses himself to those still concerned about biblical injunctions about women, Richard Norris to those to whom the 'maleness' of Christ is still a major issue, and John Austin Baker to those worried about the 'rightness' of the time. Fr Eric Doyle gives us a wise and most helpful summary of the Roman Catholic position.

It may be significant that women writers have tended to occupy themselves with quite different areas of the debate from those mentioned above. Janet Morley writes about the language of the Alternative Service Book with its unconscious revelation of attitudes which need to be recognized and changed. Mary Tanner writes of the many women today painfully testing their vocations. Jill Robson, another Roman Catholic, writes about Mariolatry, and Jane Williams compares Jewish attitudes to women at the time of Jesus with the very different demands he appeared to make of them in terms of life and growth. Anne Hoad writes of a new understanding of priesthood: 'Today's concept of priesthood has arisen from an historical process evolving within greatly varying cultures, many of which held a very limited and sometimes hostile view of women.' Henriette Santer, writing as a clinical psychologist, indicates how stereotypes of men and women have blinded and restricted us all, but shows how such stereotypes are themselves breaking down as a result of new insights.

Rowan Williams, in a movingly argued essay about ministry, suggests that the life of Jesus was a kind of judgement upon all who wished to dominate and who would not share power. 'Man as wielder-of-power is judged by the God whose embodiment among us refuses that sort of authority, and in some sense may be said to have spoken for the cause of women, as he speaks for all victims.'

Peter Clark, writing on behalf of the MOW Theology Group,

which worked collectively on the material for their essay,
struggles with the problem of hierarchy and suggests that the
task is to see

> all our hierarchies not as *God-given* . . . but as provisional.
> Furthermore we must learn to see them as the place in which we are
> to strive towards the possibility of a non-hierarchical under-
> standing of our world . . . Openness, adaptability, might be said to
> be the key-notes of the shift away from a hierarchical under-
> standing of the nature of society. The ability to listen, to hold a
> silence, to meet people where they are, to admit that one might be
> mistaken, to receive forgiveness where it is offered as well as to
> offer it where it is needed – these would be the characteristics of a
> life redeemed from hierarchy.

The issue of the ordination of women does, clearly, raise many
related issues about ministry. It raises, too, questions about the
way women have, until recently, been excluded from all
positions of status and decision-making in the Church. (My
impression as a young convert in the nineteen-fifties was that
there was little for them to do apart from ironing surplices,
making tea and arranging flowers; at my parish church they
were not even allowed to sing in the choir.) 'Woman' was
extravagantly admired and idealized in the person of Mary, yet
ignored and snubbed in the persons of living women.

Which brings me, more logically than you might imagine, to
the title of this book. *Feminine in the Church* is a title which,
even among Christian friends, caused raised eyebrows and
anxious ruminations when we first suggested it. 'Feminine' it
was felt, suggested something frilly, frivolous, and less than
serious. It was uncomfortably close to 'effeminate', in our
society an adjective invariably used as an insult. 'Feminine' had
a soft, dependent, helpless connotation, and this seemed a
dangerous implication when we are claiming that women have
gifts, powers, strengths, which the Church is seriously
neglecting.

Two things finally drove us to decide on the title in spite of its
drawbacks. One was that it was extraordinarily piquant; the
juxtaposition of the words 'feminine' and 'Church' gave the
reader a start, a kind of *frisson*, which was in itself a revealing

reaction. The words seemed to lie uneasily alongside one another, even, in combination, to be faintly shocking. The shock, it seemed to us, might be salutary, since it made a point for us – that something deeply embedded in human nature, represented by half the human race and more than half of most Church congregations, had hitherto been felt, in some deep, puzzling sense, to be inimical to, or excluded from, the Church.

The other reason was that some of us wanted to 'own' the word 'feminine', to redeem it from any imputation of mindless frivolity, or need of special protection, and to claim it as the word that best described our particular strengths, wisdom and attitudes. Although we were sometimes accused of 'aping men', what actually interested us was trying to lift the weight of restrictions that prevented us from being as fully ourselves, as fully 'feminine', as possible. In this respect the heaviest weight and the worst restriction, in or out of the Church, was the implication that being a woman was somehow an inferior or unsatisfactory state over against the more desirable possibility of being a man. Much in Church structure, government and language contributes to this implication, quite apart from the issue of ordination, and women are requesting the Church to examine its thinking in this respect and to make its rejection of the implication entirely clear.

That this might have profound repercussions for Christian thinking about the relations between men and women, about sexuality, about power, and about much else upon which at present its mind is muddled and indecisive, would seem very likely. Perhaps if it can find its way to a happier, more honest, more just, and less sentimental, exchange between the sexes, it may find that it has more to say than it can yet imagine to a violent and frightened world in which women are often grossly abused and exploited. It will not succeed, however, without becoming conscious of the ancient and destructive fear which remains at the heart of its practice.

MONICA FURLONG
MOVEMENT FOR THE ORDINATION OF WOMEN

ONE

Women and the Ministry: A Case for Theological Seriousness

Rowan Williams

The theology of Christian ministry is an area in which we are too readily tempted to avoid discussion of first principles. It is too complicated,[1] too generally unsettling and too distracting when we are hard-pressed by practical urgencies. The result is that the Church's debating and decision-making, on internal and ecumenical matters alike, becomes sterile and polarized (I am thinking primarily of my own church, but I expect others in other contexts will share something of this perception). There are quite a few who would say that, at the moment, a theology of (ordained) ministry is neither possible nor desirable: we have inherited a jumble of rather irrational structures and practices which we are slowly – and *pragmatically* – learning to adjust and rationalize or even modernize; and in this sort of situation, we are inevitably going to treat all theological perspectives on ministry as provisional. The corollary, which some would draw out in so many words, is that, if we don't know theologically just what ministry is, there can be no good theological reasons for *not* doing anything that looks attractive in practical terms. Over against this stands what appears to be a complex, sophisticated and self-assured theology of the nature of priestly ministry, insisting upon the *responsibility* of theology to the data of revelation and on the need for what might be called a christological control upon the Church's practice. We have no business to regard the Church's theology of ministry as provisional: like all else in the Church, it is under the judgement of the Incarnate Word. If the ordained minister is not to be reduced to the level of a professional manager or administrator, or even *just* a delegate of the Christian congregation, we need a firmer grounding for our theological vision in our under-

11

standing of the person of Christ. If Christ exercises no control on our theologizing, then we had better admit that we have abandoned any attempt at continuity with mainstream Christian tradition.[2]

As a matter of fact, I believe it is important to recognize that this polarity is real enough. If we had to choose between a Church tolerably confident of what it has to say and seeking only for effective means of saying it, and a Church constantly engaged in an internal dialogue and critique of itself, an exploration to discover what is central to its being, I should say that it is the latter which is the more authentic - a Church which understands that part of what it is *offering* to humanity is the possibility of living in such a mode. What the Church 'has to say' is never a simple verbal message: it is an invitation to entrust your life to a certain vision of the possibilities of humanity in union with God. And to entrust yourself in this way is to put your thinking and experience, your reactions and your initiatives daily into question, under the judgement of the central creative memory of Jesus Christ, present in his Spirit to his community. When objectors to the ordination of women to the priesthood insist that the Church must make sure that it has built into it aspects of its life and order which keep it attentive to the priority of revealed truth in Jesus, I agree entirely with the implied concern.

This is sometimes expressed in terms of the need for the Church to represent to itself Christ as Head or as Bridegroom - as the *source* of its intelligible life and unity, as partner in a relationship aiming at fertility. We should not think simply in terms of a charism of leadership or co-ordination,[3] but of something which 'ministers' to the Church the remembrance that Christ is not a part of *its* life, that the Church exists because of an initiative outside itself which it never assimilates or masters.[4] This is superbly summed up in some words of Hans Urs von Balthasar (I retain his masculine pronouns!):

This is the first quality that the priest I am looking for would have to have; for he would have to be a priest, or at any rate he would have to have been commissioned and authorized from above, by Christ, to confront me with God's incarnate word in such a

12

manner that I can be sure that it is not I who am making use of it; I have to know that I have not from the very outset emasculated it by psychologizing, interpreting, demythologizing it away to such an extent that it can no longer create in me what it wills.[5]

I want to suggest in this essay that it is possible to see this kind of understanding of public ministry in the Church as actually pressing *towards* the ordination of women to the priesthood rather than otherwise; and that if those eager to see women exercising priestly ministry were concerned to develop a theology of ministry which took such considerations seriously, it just might be possible for the present deadlock in debate to be broken a little - if only because it would make it plain that the issue between proponents and opponents of the priesthood of women is not *necessarily* to do with 'fidelity to the doctrine of the incarnation'[6] or to the sense of the Church's existence 'under judgement'.[7]

When we find in the gospels the commissions from Jesus to the apostles (Matthew 16.19; 18.18; John 20.22-3) empowering them to act as something like judges in the rabbinical courts, we are reminded that the early Christian communities made an allowance for the exercise of a disciplinary power recalling believers to faithfulness. This is obvious enough from the epistles of Paul and John and the writer to the Hebrews, but what is important in the gospel passages is the immediate association of this with the primary apostolic commission. The apostolate, the foundational ministry for the community, by which the resurrection witness continues to break through human frontiers to create a new and united humanity, is also a ministry of discernment and discrimination *within* the community. It is empowered to 'retain' sin as well as to remit it: to declare to the Church its unfaithfulness to its calling, its unconvertedness. If the apostolate is, under God, what draws together the community of faith and equips it to continue the mission and ministry of Christ in the world, it must also be what keeps alive the question of the community's integrity, by challenging its practice in the name of the gospel – to which, of course, the apostolate is no less answerable.

A Church concerned about its integrity will be concerned that there are those who minister to it in this way – by a witness of edification and criticism together, a ministry pressing the question, 'What sort of community is this meant to be?', at the same moment in which it summons the community to active loyalty to Christ in the world. This can (and should) be said without binding us to simplistic ideas of the absolute identity of character and office between the Twelve and the ordained ministry of later generations, let alone to the conviction that the 'historic threefold ministry' or anything like it was consciously envisaged and deliberately constituted by Jesus of Nazareth.[8] What matters is rather that we understand that we have no knowledge of a Church without 'apostolic' ministering at its heart; how that apostolic service was first organized and transmitted, we can have little or no certainty. The 'institution-alizing' of this ministry by the end of the first century was, however, not just a betrayal of primitive liberty (though no such step ever occurs without some of the ambiguity of all political process[9]); as soon as the question is raised of *public* criteria for recognizing the continuing identity of a community (the question, 'How do we know we're still engaged in the same project/conversation/way of life?'), some considerations about institutionalized succession are bound to come in. Schillebeeckx puts it concisely:

> A community without a good, matter-of-fact pastoral institution-alization of its ministry (a development of it in changed circumstances) runs the risk of losing for good the apostolicity and thus ultimately the Christian character of its origin, inspiration and orientation – and in the last resort its own identity. Ministry is connected with a special concern for the preservation of the Christian identity of the community in constantly changing circumstances.[10]

And Balthasar characteristically asks: 'How could a Christian who remains ever a sinner have the confidence to guarantee his or her complete ecclesiastical obedience on the basis of purely charismatic order . . .?'[11] – which is not to say that ordained

14

ministry is a system for securing conformity (however easily it is distorted into that), but that our 'obedience' to Christ and his gospel, our response, our attention, our willingness to be shaped and changed by it and not to lose sight of it in the vicissitudes of history, is more than a question of private conviction. Living our Christian lives with a measure of self-trust and authority involves being part of a 'public' process, aware of itself and its history; the institutionalizing of ministry (like the formation of the canon of Scripture) has, from very early on, been a vital part of that historical self-awareness which (in an ideal world!) should serve or empower the authority of believing women and men, and deliver them from the tyrannies of individual feeling and unspoken, unchecked manipulation (by me or by others), and in this sense is clearly pastoral as well as prophetic.

If this is correct, the 'apostolic' ministry is that ministry whose special province is both to gather the believing community around the centre which it proclaims, the preaching of the resurrection, and *in* that gathering, to make sure that this community is critically aware of itself. The 'apostolate' is a ministry representing the fact that the Church is *called*, and is answerable for its fidelity to this call. In this sense, apostolic ministry may occur in a variety of contexts and by way of a variety of structures;[12] but Catholic Christianity (from which description I do not mean to exclude the churches of the Reformation) has held to the conviction that a faithful Church will recognize and secure certain structures defined very directly in terms of this ministry. The ordained - i.e. the 'ordered', recognized, legitimized - ministry is there, most simply, to minister to the Church's very identity.

In some traditions this ministry has been conceived primarily as a teaching office; but, to the extent that the Church ministers to its identity and its truthfulness in public worship and sacrament, and to the extent that regular or 'ordered' worship relates to the presence of the 'ordered' minister, the apostolic ministry is more than that of preacher or teacher.

Public worship is the concrete place in which the community, assembling out of its diaspora in the world, achieves and renews its real order; in that, in public worship 'it fully enacts that separation between the realms of the old and the new age which threatens to become blurred in everyday life', and in the Lord's Supper recognizes itself as the Body of Christ, and verifies its call and mission in the ever-fresh, present proclamation of the already accomplished mighty works of God (1 Peter 2.9).[13]

The minister, as focus or *animateur* of liturgy - in particular the eucharistic liturgy - is thus part of the process of the Church's self-recognition: not just as teacher or leader (in the ordinary pragmatic sense) but as a present point of reference for the Church's historical awareness and sense of responsibility to and for its calling. In *this* sense, we might cautiously speak about the ordained ministry 'representing' the Headship of Christ in the Church, and thus about the need for the relation between minister and community being one of dialogue (with its necessary distance), not only of delegated representation. This is an involved issue, raising many questions about what 'distance' is necessary, how this is balanced with the equally necessary *solidarity* with a community, and what sort of dangers there are in over-stressing the 'prophetic' dimension of ordained ministry,[14] I do not have space here to tackle all of these in anything like the detail desirable; but I hope that the following sections will suggest some possible ways of responding to such questions. For the moment, though, let what has been said so far stand as a proposal for understanding the role of the ordained ministry in a way which allows for the element of 'over-againstness' in the ordained person's relation to the Church in general.

What usually worries people when this sort of language is used is the implication (real or imagined) that there is a clerical caste in the Church, a group of Christians decisively set apart by a distinctive 'Christian culture' or spirituality, by status and privilege. Given the history of the Church, no one in their right mind could claim that this was an unjustified worry. However, we are not the first generation to feel it. In the early medieval Church, the celibacy of the clergy - strange as it may seem - had a lot to do with efforts to prevent the clerical body becoming a

16

kind of tribe, with office, wealth and privilege passing in hereditary succession; the result was, of course, a still more dramatically separate body, structurally independent of 'external' ties and loyalties. The Reformation sought to undo this by stressing an austere functionalism in the ministerial office (the 'teaching elder' model); and the result of this was the emergence of the minister-as-bourgeois-professional (on the Continent, anyway, and perhaps in Scotland; England was, as usual, much more confused, less interested in professionalism, more inclined to assimilate its clergy to the minor aristocracy and the squirearchy[15]).

The point is, that throughout the Church's history the 'otherness' and 'distance' of the person called by God through the Church to offer it words and signs for its identity, its truth to itself, is constantly assimilated to the otherness and distance of social or cultural differentiation. And if that is happening, the independence and sovereignty of God's call to the Church can come to be trapped and silenced by its association with purely contingent gulfs and differences. Worst of all, it can come to be seen as an instrument of active oppression, an ideological tool. In such circumstances, the 'apostolic' ministry has practically ceased to be apostolic in any sense: it fulfils its responsibility neither to the Church nor to the world.

We are familiar enough with this problem as it arises in connection with class divisions in Britain. The almost universal situation in which parishes in the inner city or the council estate are ministered to by clergy who are middle-class by background or education or both presents difficulties to which there are no simple and quick solutions. Fr Paul Bull of Mirfield lamented at the turn of the century that England possessed 'a class priesthood with a money qualification';[16] and although this is no longer strictly true in immediate economic terms, it remains true at the cultural level. There is plenty of impressive solidarity in action, but, in the nature of the case, it rarely grows directly out of shared experience and common social interest. The priest is still someone who has *chosen* to identify; in other words, some of the viciously divisive effects of class/cultural difference can be overcome, but there is, nonetheless, no obvious way of disentangling the necessarily distinct perspective of someone given the responsibility of speaking to a community as a whole about its integrity and the perspective possessed by someone in virtue of a more 'advantaged' upbringing, which can communicate itself as élitist and judgemental. I do not suppose we shall ever get this entirely right, certainly not in our present class-ridden social and educational structures. We can do little more than to recognize the problem candidly and to encourage any steps, however small, which help to equip a ministry rooted in its native local and social concerns, yet resistant to parochialism and capable of prophecy without merely *cultural* alienation.[17]

If we understand what the judgement of the gospel means, we are bound to recognize that the relation of liberator to liberated, saviour to saved, can never be the same as the relation of one *human group* to another. When we delude ourselves that it is, we risk taking away the gospel's power to change the relations between human persons and groups. Gradually, we have become more sensitive to this (if not more successful in dealing with it) in the sphere of the more 'obvious' sorts of human division, racial, cultural and social; we have heard enough about the dangers of identifying religion with middle-class values in this country or identifying the Church with colonialism in the mission field. These are the clichés of every Christian liberal. What I want to insist on is that this sort of perspective needs a firm theological edge if it is to be more than liberal cliché; it needs, in fact, a constant attention to the ways in which faith both informs and is activated by our experience of an unhealed or unconverted humanity, inside and outside the Church – an attention which should issue in a theology which takes seriously the importance of a continuing critical engagement with the central challenge of *revelation*, the givenness of that memory of God's Word crucified and raised, which questions and interrupts our world. And such an attention involves hard thinking about ministry and apostolicity, and a readiness to carry the critique of existing ministry into less 'obvious' areas.

So we come at last to the question of women and the ordained ministry. The analogy is clear: the gospel is no more to be bound to sexual 'otherness' than it is to any other human system of division. Here, however, the objection is raised, 'Is sexual differentiation the same sort of thing as difference of race or class or whatever?' Over some sorts of distinction between persons we have a measure of control, but not over this. Therefore (the argument runs) it would be hasty to conclude that the heavily masculine imagery of Christian tradition and the maleness of Jesus are contingent or peripheral matters; if we are here dealing with a differentiation built into the created order, is it not likely that God would use this fact as an intrinsic part of what he wills to reveal to us? Some aspects of Jesus' historical identity are unquestionably matters of indifference; but here is a fundamental either/or (the presence or absence of the Y chromosome). Is God unconcerned with this aspect of Jesus' humanity?

> A number of modern Christologists have held that there is a radical affinity between human nature and the Person of the Word. If this is so, may it not be that not only the humanity of Jesus but also the sexual mode under which he assumed it reflects a real aspect of the eternal Word? Or must we say, on the other hand, that the eternal Word transcends the particularity of his incarnate maleness *in precisely the same way* as he transcends the particularity of his incarnate first-century Palestinian Jewishness?[18]

Remarks like this are almost always followed by reassurances that this has nothing to do with questions of power or superiority. We are speaking *only* of symbolic functions.[19] Now I don't believe these reassurances are dishonest, or even that the whole argument is contemptible rationalization; there are important worries being aired about the theological significance of the *particular*, the concrete historicity of God's speech with us in Jesus.[20] But there is a good deal more to be said, and I shall try to say at least some of it in the last few pages of this essay.

1. The male-female polarity is genetically determined.[21] So are other human differences at the biological level. It is a mistake to assume instantly that this difference is (because of its undeniably important nature, practically and symbolically) of

another order entirely. In other words, it is one of a number of biological 'givens'; and, as with others, its role in determining behaviour or personality structure is unclear. We should tread cautiously here, as the debates surrounding this sort of question are vastly wide-ranging. But it should be enough to note that it is possible to say that Jesus' *biological* maleness is not theologically all-important without suggesting either that the particularity of his humanity is of no interest (and there are, after all, other genetic facts about him that we pay no attention to) or that sexual differentiation is of no anthropological concern or is a matter of culture and socialization or is wholly under our control, etc.

2. In the world as it actually is, we do not find biological male–female polarity existing in a social vacuum. Women and men do not have only 'biological' relations, so to speak. Their difference is deeply bound up in speech and culture, it has been mythologized and institutionalized, it expresses itself in terms of power, dependence and independence, *economics*.[22] It is essential to realize this: talk of symbolic function based on 'natural distinction', which ignores the *facts* of human social relations, is dangerously naive. It is a matter of fact that nearly all arguments in theology appealing to the order of nature on this matter have been constructed in the context of male domination, i.e. they are not ideologically innocent. The same is almost bound to be true of arguments based on symbolism in the societies we know. 'Natural differences can only come to mean social inequality in an unequal society';[23] 'symbolic' differences run the same risk.

This may sound harsh. But I do not mean to suggest that symbols are either unimportant or oppressive. On the contrary, it is because they *are* so important and have such creative potential that we need to see as clearly as we can what they mean and how they work in the actual historical circumstances we find ourselves in. It is always tempting to think that we who 'operate' the symbols control their meaning. But we have learned, in the Church, how little this is true: generations of instruction on infant baptism have not broken through a set of often extraordinarily non-Christian ('para-Christian'?) ideas

20

and expectations in the minds of most people. And a decision to cut this Gordian knot by operating a highly selective and rigorist policy is also to make a symbolic statement we don't control – often a statement heard and experienced as élitist and exclusive, particularly by those who are already feeling marginal, powerless, shut out.

If we use symbols, we must learn to cope with their uncomfortable uncontrollability and to live with the consequences of using them. If we want to argue the 'women's issue' in symbolic terms, we need to see what we are doing in the society we are in. Intentions apart, what if the real effect of such a symbolic argument is to reinforce patterns of inequality and/or to produce deep hurt and alienation? What if this makes it harder for women (real and particular women) to belong in the Church, to see it as a community of liberty or reconciliation? What if it is heard simply to echo what is heard in the world, a systematic devaluing of human female experience? *Of course* we are talking about individual or 'subjective' perceptions and responses here; but these are part of the Church's pastoral agenda. There is at least a strong case for saying that this kind of language and symbolism, stressing the centrality of Christ's masculinity, makes it impossible for many people not otherwise spectacularly silly or wicked to hear the Word of God, because it ignores their real and present human situation. If God designed it so that the maleness of Jesus expressed a basic symbolic structure, and straightforwardly revealed some vital fact about the divine, he did so in the context of a heavily patriarchal society: is it not inevitable that, if we think in these terms, we shall present a God who endorses that kind of society? – unless we ascribe to God an unconcern with the practical outworking of symbolism comparable to that of some of his theological witnesses.

3. The idea that the relation of men to the humanity of Jesus is different from that of women is a corollary of the 'symbolic' argument, and a rather odd and unorthodox one. The point has been made[24] that the patristic conviction of the Word's assumption of humanity-as-such in the incarnation leaves little room for such a differentiation. Even the most rampantly

misogynistic of the Fathers do not suggest outright that women are 'in Christ' otherwise than men. The notion of celibate women acquiring honorary maleness in their virtue is found here and there, but not given a christological grounding.[25]

What is more, if we go back to my earlier point, the necessity of not identifying the liberator-liberated relation with the relation between any two human groups, we have an enormous difficulty in the suggestion that men and women relate differently to the person of the liberator. How could this ever be expressed in terms that did not imply that femaleness is a bondage from which the male (unilaterally and not mutually) liberates?

4. Part of the problem here stems from the fact that the relation of the man Jesus to the Word and the Father is seen as a kind of simple 'linear' manifestation. Some feminist theologians have explored the idea that the maleness of Jesus might matter in another way. Perhaps, it is suggested, only a male representative of God could in his person and his fate so *challenge* the assumption of a kinship between the masculine power structures of the world and the power of God to liberate women and men alike from the tyranny of patriarchal authority. Rosemary Ruether speaks of a 'kenosis of patriarchy',[26] Angela West describes the story of Jesus as a memory which 'presents God as the ultimate contradiction to the worship of male power, and mocks all gods and goddesses, who are nothing more than this'.[27]

If this is a viable theological idea, its force is that Jesus' maleness is important because, as a *crucified* or *marginal* or *powerless* maleness, it represents as dramatically as possible the 'otherness' and the judgement of God's Word upon the world's patterns of dominance. It does not manifest but subverts the 'maleness' of God. Its symbolic importance is not in being a timeless image but in its pertinence to specific social forms. Thus it does not imply different levels or kinds of ontological relationship between women, men, and the Word Incarnate; it makes the same point as is made by saying that, while God in Christ identifies with all human beings, this identification becomes a critical and challenging matter when grasped in relation to the poor and the rejected. It is not that the poor are ontologically more God-like, but that their cause is made to be God's own. To see God's relation to or solidarity with the poor is to see the tragedy and inhumanity of poverty. If God, the God of liberty and fulfilment, is 'with' the poor, it can only be as the impetus to a protesting hope, because of the experienced contradiction between liberty-and-fulfilment and the actual condition of poverty. So with the meaning of Jesus' maleness; God is not shown more womanlike than manlike by the humiliation and death of Jesus (which would then turn into a kind of revenge fantasy), man-in-the-abstract is not judged more severely than woman-in-the-abstract. But man-as-wielder-of-power *is* judged by the God whose embodiment among us refuses that sort of authority, and in some sense may be said to have spoken for the cause of women, as he speaks for all victims (but also in his actual practice as remembered by the Church).

This is a scheme which needs more development and clarification, certainly; but it is a highly significant response to the accusation that the priestly ordination of women demands a theology which neglects the humanity of Jesus. Here the contours of Jesus' historical identity (including his maleness) are central, but not in a way which could provide justification for a continuation of male-centred symbolism of the undialectical, iconic kind defended by the opponents of women's ordination. The *last* thing you can do with the maleness of Jesus on this account is to abstract to its biological essence and turn it into a theoretical basis for uncontroverted male power-and-symbol structures.

5. A final, related point: I have argued that ordained ministry is there to address the unfulfilment and unconvertedness of the Church, to speak to the Church in the name of the Kingdom. It needs therefore to speak to the Church on behalf of the poor and excluded – and specifically of those whom the Church itself *causes* to be 'poor and excluded', to feel devalued, rejected or dehumanized. Can this be done with any credibility if the ordained ministry expresses no solidarity with such people? And these are questions not only about women, or homo-

sexuals, or divorcees, but about all whose history is marked down by the Church as failure, whose experience is sealed off from the exercise of 'professional pastoring'. This, if anything, is the way to make pastoral ministry dramatically unprophetic.

The preceding section is, in a way, a long parenthesis. If the point is accepted that a ministry which ministers the transcendent and paradoxical power of the Word of God in Jesus must never be identified structurally with purely worldly forms of differentiation, it should be obvious that restricted access to this ministry is a contradiction, which risks turning God into a thing in the world, transcendence into contingent strangeness. (It's like the assumption that worship which conveys 'the transcendent' *must* be dominated by what is contingently, culturally, strange; I entirely accept the role of the 'strange' in good and imaginative worship, but should hesitate to identify the presence of any one form of it with a direction towards the transcendent.) However, a good many people have an anxiety – not necessarily stupid or frivolous – that the assimilation of sexual differentiation to other kinds of distinction opens the door to some sort of disregard for God's purposes as expressed in history and the flesh. This anxiety needs hearing and answering, and I have tried to contribute something towards an answer. Those who have linked this anxiety with theories about the symbolic importance of Jesus' maleness have, on the whole, made the link in a fairly tentative and exploratory way, and this encourages me to think that a reply is worthwhile: there *might* be a conversation to continue. Perhaps I am too sanguine. All the same, if a book or an essay on this topic is worth writing at all, it must be in the hope that we have not yet completely stopped listening to each other in the Church.

Notes

1. The literature on the theology of ministry is notoriously vast. T.F. O'Meara, *Theology of Ministry* (New York, Paulist Press, 1983), lists some surveys on p. 211.

2. This sort of argument is stated in a number of the contributions to P. Moore (ed.), *Man, Woman and Priesthood*, SPCK, 1978. See especially the papers by E.L. Mascall, Kallistos Ware, and Gilbert Russell and Margaret Dewey.

3. O'Meara (op. cit., ch. 6) occasionally comes near to saying this; and cf. E. Schillebeeckx, *Ministry: A Case for Change* (SCM, 1981), pp. 134-9. But both writers make it very clear that they are not simply using pragmatic or 'worldly' notions of leadership. For some critical remarks on 'leadership' from a feminist viewpoint, see Sara Maitland, *A Map of the New Country* (Routledge and Kegan Paul, 1983), p. 121.

4. Cf. my *Resurrection: Interpreting the Easter Gospel* (Darton Longman and Todd, 1982), ch. 4, for further reflections on this.

5. H.U. von Balthasar, *Elucidations* (SPCK, 1975), p. 107 (from an essay on 'The priest I want').

6. Many critics of feminist theology seem to think that the work of a radical 'post-Christian' separatist like Mary Daly is typical or normative or the inevitable implication of a commitment to the ordination of women. Even a cursory acquaintance with what is actually being said and written by feminist theologians should show how mistaken this assumption is.

7. I should perhaps add that, as I want to address the theological points at issue, I have said nothing about the so-called 'practical' or 'ecumenical' arguments. I believe that the onus of proof is on those who claim that such considerations ought to outweigh *positive* theological reasons for change.

8. On the complex points at issue here, E. Schweizer, *Church Order in the New Testament* (SCM, 1961), remains one of the best guides available. Part 1, A, section 2 deals with Jesus' own aims.

9. Graham Shaw, *The Cost of Authority* (SCM, 1982), is sobering reading (even if grotesquely overstated at times) on the manipulative power-politics sometimes discernible behind NT texts.

10. Schillebeeckx, op. cit., p. 24.

11. From an essay in *Pneuma and Institution*, Einsiedeln, 1974; quoted from *The von Balthasar Reader*, ed. M. Kehl and W. Löser (T. & T. Clark, 1983), p. 272.

12. A point which Barth used as part of his polemical insistence on the dangers of established clerical 'order' of any kind. See his discussion in *Church Dogmatics* IV.2, T. & T. Clark.

13. Gerhard Bauer, 'Karl Barths Vorstellungen von der Ordnung der Gemeinde und die kirchlichen Ordungen der EKiD', in *Theologie zwischen Gestern und Morgen: Interpretationen und Anfragen zum Werk Karl Barths*, ed. W. Dantine and K. Lüthi (Munich, Kaiser Verlag, 1968), p. 141. The quotation in the text is from Schweizer, op. cit., Part 2, section 27.

14. However, I am hesitant about endorsing the distinction between 'pastoral' and 'prophetic' ministry uncritically. 'Pastoral' means more than 'consolatory', 'prophetic' more than 'unsettling'.

15. In chapter 83 of Trollope's *Last Chronicle of Barset*, Mr Crawley reports Archdeacon Grantly's acknowledgement of, not a shared priestly ministry, but a common social status. '"We stand", said he, "on the only perfect level on which such men can meet each other. We are both gentlemen."'

16. G.L. Prestige, *The Life of Charles Gore* (Heinemann, 1935), p. 218.

17. The experience of the emergence of something like a genuinely locally-rooted priestly ministry in the (Anglican) Episcopal Area of Stepney in the 1970s is one such small but encouraging sign.

18. E.L. Mascall, *Whatever Happened to the Human Mind?* (SPCK, 1980), p. 146.

19. Fr Mascall refers to the speculative and brilliantly ingenious essay of Père Louis Bouyer, *Mystère et ministères de la femme* (Paris, Aubier, 1976), for further suggestions about symbolism; though even he admits that P. Bouyer is rather hermetic at times.

20. For what it's worth, I should perhaps say that these were the considerations which for several years prevented me from supporting the ordination of women to the priesthood. I have not changed my mind about their importance but about their implications.

21. In one obvious sense (the presence or absence of the Y chromosome). But the relation between genetic, gonadal and genital sexual differentiation is far from simple: 'biology' means more than genetics. For a clear and useful survey of the question, see *Women and Sex Roles: A Social Psychological Perspective*, by Irene H. Frieze, Jacquelynne E. Parsons, Paula B. Johnson, Diane N. Ruble and Gail L. Zellman (New York, Norton, 1978), pp. 83-94.

22. Various studies in Kate Young, Carol Wolkowitz, Roslyn McCullagh (eds.), *Of Marriage and the Market: Women's Subordination in International Perspective*, CSE Books, 1981.

23. ibid., p. 39, from an essay by Verena Stolcke on 'Women's Labours: the Naturalization of Social Inequality and Women's Subordination'.

24. Authoritatively by Richard Norris, see essay no. 5.

25. On patristic attitudes, see Rosemary Radford Ruether, 'Misogynism and Virginal Feminism in the Fathers of the Church', in *Religion and Sexism: Images of Woman in the Jewish and Christian Traditions*, ed. R.R. Ruether, New York, Simon and Schuster, 1974.

26. *Sexism and God-Talk: Toward a Feminist Theology* (Boston, Beacon Press/London, SCM Press, 1983), pp. 134-8.

27. 'A Faith for Feminists', in *Walking on the Water: Women Talk About Spirituality*, ed. Jo Garcia and Sara Maitland (Virago, 1983), p. 88.

TWO

The Ordination of Women in the Roman Catholic Church

Eric Doyle, OFM

The subject on which I have been invited to make some remarks is the actual state of the question in the Roman Catholic Church about the ordination of women to the ministerial priesthood. In approaching the subject, I set myself this precise question: Is it still a question in the Roman Catholic Church? The aim of these pages is to examine the data at hand in order to arrive at an exact and unemotional answer to that question. I add 'unemotional' deliberately, because the issue about the ordination of women is an emotive one. When it is raised, emotions run high and they run riot. So often on both sides the wish is father to the thought. While intuitions and insights cannot be despised, they have to be tested, and this is as applicable methodologically in theology as it is in physics.

This, then, is the question being asked: Is the ordination of women to the ministerial priesthood still a question in the Roman Catholic Church? *De facto* of course the question is being debated among Roman Catholics, as experience shows. But what of the *de iure* situation? Is it legitimate in the Roman Catholic Church to raise and discuss the question and even to hold the view that women can be ordained? This question about legitimacy derives its importance from the fact that the Congregation for the Doctrine of the Faith published on 15 October 1976 a Declaration, known from its opening latin words *Inter insigniores*, concerning the question of the admission of women to the ministerial priesthood. The answer appears already in the final paragraph of the Declaration's introduction: 'The Sacred Congregation for the Doctrine of the Faith judges it necessary to recall that the Church, in fidelity to the example of the Lord, does not consider herself authorized to admit women to priestly ordination.'[1]

The Declaration came from a mandate of Pope Paul VI. He then approved and confirmed it and ordered it to be published. One might be inclined to conclude from these circumstances especially, that the question is definitively and irrevocably closed. But, as we shall see, this is a conclusion that cannot be drawn.

What, then, is the doctrinal status of the Declaration? What kind of authority does it possess? The answer to this question requires some analysis of the complex machinery that lies behind statements from Rome. While this may seem a little tedious, it is necessary in order to be able to assess the specific status and weight of the Declaration, and I ask the reader's indulgence for what follows.

The Declaration is no merely private statement presented by a group of Roman theologians. It comes from the Congregation for the Doctrine of the Faith (known formerly as the Holy Office) and it is a document concerning the content of Christian revelation.

The Pope frequently exercises his non-infallible, ordinary teaching office through the Roman congregations. He may approve a decree or a declaration of a congregation in a solemn way, in which case he makes the entire document his own and promulgates it in his own name. On the other hand, he may approve a decree or a declaration in a general way and in that case he confirms it as a document of the respective congregation. This latter type of approval is by far the more common, and decrees or declarations thus approved remain entirely the work of the congregation involved. In this case such documents cannot be infallible, because the Pope cannot delegate the infallible teaching office.

It is the responsibility of the Congregation for the Doctrine of the Faith to safeguard the Church's teaching on faith and morals. The authority of its declarations does not derive from the convincing power or weight of the arguments produced for a particular position, but from its participation in the teaching office of the Pope. Thus, the Declaration on the admission of women to the ministerial priesthood is a highly authoritative document which deserves great respect and is to be examined with gravity. In terms of the position it adopts, no Roman Catholic woman may be ordained to the priesthood, nor may any Roman Catholic attempt to procure the ordination of a woman.

Nevertheless, when all this has been said, it has to be pointed out that the Declaration is not an infallible pronouncement. It is not, in the words of the definition of papal infallibility, 'of itself irreformable',[2] nor does it possess the certitude that excludes all fear of error. The question about women priests, therefore, is not definitively and irrevocably closed in the Roman Catholic Church. The fact of papal approval and confirmation does not alter this, precisely because the Declaration remains entirely the work of the congregation.

To anyone familiar with the history of Roman pronouncements this is nothing new or remarkable. The Roman Catholic Church and Roman Catholic theology have long known the distinction between irreformable definitions of the Roman magisterium and authoritative though reformable pronouncements. The Church is an essentially historical reality and various factors - political, sociological, psychological and theological - come into play when a decree or declaration is made.

In respect of the present Declaration, it seems to be the case that, while there is a very significant and articulate minority in the Roman Catholic Church which holds that there is no doctrinal or theological objection to the ordination of women and that it is intrinsically desirable that women should be ordained, the majority are either opposed or indifferent to the ordination of women. Many people are simply not prepared psychologically or theologically even to discuss it. That, I suppose, could have been said about vernacular in the liturgy in the early 1950s.

In any case, no one at present can conclude that women are barred forever by the law of God from becoming priests. The Declaration is an authoritative but not definitive statement on the matter of admitting women to the ministerial priesthood. For this reason the discussion about the ordination of women in the Roman Catholic Church is not only not excluded, but it is imperative that it be continued.

Theology's task is not simply one of repetition. Even in regard to the explicit teachings of divine and catholic faith, the theologian expounds and unfolds the meanings contained in them, establishes the relationship of one truth to another and demonstrates how any particular statement of faith is to be understood in the light of the Church's faith as such. Therefore, in regard to authoritative documents of the Roman magisterium which are not definitive or infallible, it is much less the case that the theologian should simply repeat them or necessarily justify them. The doctrinal reason for this is that the authority of faith derives from the authority of the Word of God itself, to which the magisterium is a servant.

In a very balanced study of the question published after the Declaration, Fr John Wijngaards, MHM, explains the doctrinal status of the Declaration as follows:

> According to generally accepted ecclesiastical interpretation such doctrinal declarations by the Congregation do not impede further discussion. In at least two official interpretations given, it was authoritatively stated that such documents 'have not in the least the aim to forbid that Catholic writers should study the question further and, after carefully weighing the arguments on both sides, adhere to the contrary opinion'. (2 June 1927)[3]

This quotation is taken from a declaration of the Holy Office in connection with a reply which the Holy Office itself had given on 13 January 1897, concerning the Johannine Comma. Though Wijngaards does not quote it, the text goes on to say 'provided that they own themselves ready to stand by the Church's decision, which has received from Jesus Christ the authority not only to interpret Scripture but also to safeguard it faithfully'. Nevertheless, the Holy Office did not forbid scholars to hold the opposite view with regard to the Johannine Comma, namely that 1 John 5.7b,c–8a, is a marginal gloss that crept into the text of the Old Latin and Vulgate texts of the New Testament.

Wijngaards also gives a quotation from a letter to Cardinal Suhard from the secretary of the Biblical Commission, on the Mosaic authorship of the Pentateuch and on the historical character of Genesis 1—11, published on 16 January 1948. The quotation reads: '. . . such decisions do in no way oppose the further and really scientific study of such questions'.[4] Though both these official interpretations refer to scriptural questions, Wijngaards explains: 'It was generally agreed, even before Vatican II, that this interpretation should be extended to all documents of the same kind and that by their very nature, these documents do not exclude further discussion.'[5] In support of this position he refers the reader to the work of Fr Francis Sullivan, SJ on the Church, where Sullivan equiparates decrees of the Holy Office and replies from the Biblical Commission.[6] Even the manualists admitted that the assent to be given to decrees of the Holy See is relative and conditional.[7]

In an address given nearly twenty years ago under the title 'The position of women in the new situation in which the Church finds herself' Fr Karl Rahner maintained:

> . . . there can be no real point or prospect of achieving anything by pursuing this question [women and the priesthood] at this point in the history of the Church's understanding of her own faith and of her practice outside the specialist circles of those engaged in scientific theology. Nor is it of any avail to point to the developments in theology and in actual practice with regard to this question which have taken place among Evangelical Christians. For these do not in fact recognize any official priesthood based on sacramental consecration such as provides the basis for the fundamental distinction between clergy and people.[8]

This passage calls for some comment. Much has happened in the two decades since Rahner wrote those words. The question has been discussed at very many levels 'outside the specialist circles of those engaged in scientific theology'; indeed theology has been done in many new places.[9] Perhaps this is one of the reasons which explain the rather different view expressed by Rahner in 1972. He wrote then:

> In this connection, of course, the question might be raised whether today or at least tomorrow, in the light of the secular social situation, a woman could be considered just as much as a man for leadership of a basic community and therefore could be ordained to the priestly office. Having in mind the society of today and even

more of tomorrow, I see no reason in principle to give a negative answer to this question.[10]

Rahner, of course, was not opposed to the ordination of women when he delivered the above-mentioned address in June 1964. The point I want to emphasize is that he has clearly shifted his position on the opportuneness of the question. It should also be noted that in the course of the address he also pointed out, in passing, that in many instances those who put forward the theological arguments to support the impossibility of women priests 'are unconsciously and without realizing it working from positions deriving from an age which is no longer with us and with which we no longer need to identify ourselves'.[11]

Some qualification is required on what he says about the significance of what has taken place among Evangelical Christians. To say that it is of no avail to point to the developments which have taken place among these because they do not recognize any official priesthood, is far too general a statement. Professor J.-J. von Allmen, the Calvinist theologian, criticizes Catholic theologians who assume that this view of the ministry is held indiscriminately by all Protestants.[12] Professor von Allmen's view is that the ministry is of the *esse* of the Church and requires more than baptism for its reception and practice. Von Allmen, incidentally, is opposed to the ordination of women.

It is noteworthy also that Rahner in an essay published after the Declaration from the Congregation for the Doctrine of the Faith on the question of admitting women to the ministerial priesthood, maintains that,

> despite papal approval, the Declaration is not a definitive decision; it is in principle reformable and it can (that is not to say *a priori* that it must) be erroneous . . . the discussion is not yet at an end and it cannot consist merely in a defence of the basic thesis and arguments of the Declaration.[13]

At this point it is opportune, I think, to say something about the ecumenical significance of the doctrinal status of the Declaration. I have in mind particularly those of my Anglican brethren who are opposed to the ordination of women and who invoke the Declaration as a grave warning to the Anglican Communion. I have heard Anglicans who are opposed to the ordination of women, argue that unilateral action in ordaining women on the part of some churches of the Anglican Communion has placed an almost, if not totally insurmountable barrier across the road to Christian unity. Some even lament that by ordaining women the Anglicans have done irreparable damage to the cause of ecumenism, and they quote the Roman Declaration in support of their case.

With respect, I submit that this attitude is a little simplistic, alarmist and lacking in trust in the Holy Spirit. In response, it has to be urged that the Declaration has not closed the question definitively. While I do not consider that this will alter the view of anyone opposed to the ordination of women, I do hope it will make them cautious about using the Declaration in support of their position against those of their Anglican brethren who hold the view that women can be ordained. The ecumenical significance of the Declaration is precisely that it is not irrevocable and definitive.

But there are more important issues at stake here. Ecumenism concerns the Church of Christ as it is now making its way into a God-willed, though to us unknown, future. What is required of all of us is complete openness to the inspiration and guidance of the Holy Spirit who searches everything, even the depths of God (1 Corinthians 2.10). Moreover, the question about the ordination of women is not an isolated one. It belongs to the context of a much wider question concerning the theology of ministry. As N. Mitchell has emphasized, 'the theology of ordained ministry is, then, a derivative of ecclesiology, not vice versa'.[14] It needs to be stressed also that the ministerial priesthood is not exhaustively defined by its cultic functions, though these are an essential part of it. It includes also the preaching of the Word, teaching and leadership in the community. The ministry in general is undergoing a transformation which has already proved that the Church needs the male/female partnership in fulfilling her mission of salvation. What is most crucial, then, in the question about the ordination of women to the priesthood is the developing theology of ministry.

It must be clear to the Anglicans that there is no consensus or unanimity in the Roman Catholic Church on this question. Until very recently it was accepted that only a male can be validly ordained a priest. Since this position was *a priori* in possession, there could be no really serious question about the ordination of women. As the Declaration itself admits: '. . . we are dealing with a debate which classical theology scarcely touched on . . .'[15] Now, however, questions have arisen about the principles on which this *a priori* position is based. To ask today: 'Can a woman be ordained a priest?' is to ask a very different question than that which was asked by the Fathers of the Church or the medieval Scholastics. The difference derives from theological (especially ecclesiological), biblical, socio-logical, psychological and ecumenical factors. There is not space to examine these again here, but it is not necessary as they are well known. The new data which these diverse areas have produced about many topics in the Church have undermined and in some cases totally demolished so much that was once thought to be part of the unchanging and unchangeable nature of things. It is clear that the question about women priests that we are asking is entirely new, stemming from an altogether unprecedented understanding of the dignity, value and unique-ness of being a woman. In ecumenical terms, then, I would want to ask those of my Anglican brethren who are opposed to the ordination of women: 'Did you ever consider it distinctly possible that the growing awareness of the place of women in the Church, and the view that women can be ordained, have come about by the grace of the Holy Spirit who leads us into the truth and who is the Spirit of all times in the history of the Church?'

Finally, on this matter, I would concede to my Anglican brethren who are opposed to the ordination of women that none of us can ignore the official position of the Roman Catholic Church, the Orthodox Church and the Old Catholic Church of the Utrecht Union, on this matter. And undoubtedly there are problems here – though I do not think they are insuperable. But I would also add that the action taken by some churches of the Anglican Communion and the statement made by the General Synod cannot be ignored either. We have to be completely open to the Holy Spirit who may well be teaching us all through the Anglican Communion something very new and profound about the ministry and the role of women in it.

The Declaration, then, has not definitively closed the question about the ordination of women. I must admit that it came as something of a surprise to me that Rome chose to issue only a *declaration*.

The year before it was published I had been a member of the Sixth Anglican/Roman Catholic Working Group for (Continental) West Europe, which met in Assisi at the Centro Ecumenico from 10-14 November 1975 to consider the question of the ordination of women in the light of recent developments in this area in the Anglican Communion. The Old Catholic Church of the Utrecht Union was also represented. Peter Staples, an Anglican theologian, gave a paper on what a theologian can say about the ordination of women. Fr Nickel explained the Old Catholic viewpoint. Hervé-Marie Legrand OP and I presented theological reflections from the Roman Catholic side. All this material, together with a note appended by Canon Dessain, was edited and published by Peter Staples: *The Assisi Report 1975*, The Inter-university Institute for Missiological and Ecumenical Research, Utrecht 1975.

The Catholic representatives were present at the invitation of the Secretariat for Christian Unity. Both Legrand and myself concluded that there is no theological objection to the ordination of women. We were not, of course, stating an official position, but presenting a theological opinion. At the end of the meeting – which had been a little heated at times – there was a general feeling, by no means unanimous, that a good deal more discussion at many levels would have to take place about the ordination of women. Eleven months later, in October 1976, the Declaration was published. The gravity of the conclusion that the Church 'does not consider herself authorized to admit women to priestly ordination' might have warranted a more intrinsically authoritative document than a declaration. This is reinforced by the words of Pope Paul in his letter to the Archbishop of Canterbury, dated 30 November 1975 (only two weeks after the Working Group had met in

Assisi): 'Your Grace is of course well aware of the Catholic Church's position on this question. She holds that it is not admissible to ordain women to the priesthood, for very fundamental reasons.'[16] Yet the fact of the matter is that the Congregation for the Doctrine of the Faith issued a declaration.

Subsequently, I was invited to take part in the Anglican/ Roman Catholic Consultation on the Ordination of Women which met at Versailles from 27 February to 3 March 1978. The Anglican members were appointed by the Archbishop of Canterbury and the Secretary General of the Anglican Con- sultative Council: the Rt Revd Donald Cameron, Assistant Bishop of Sydney; the Revd Professor Edward Fasholé-Luke, Fourah Bay College, Sierra Leone; the Revd Professor James Griffiss, Nashotah House, USA; Miss Christian Howard, York; the Rt Revd Barry Valentine, Bishop of Rupert's Land, Canada, who was co-chairman; and the Revd Christopher Hill, who acted as co-secretary. The Roman Catholic members were appointed by the Vatican Secretariat for Promoting Christian Unity: Fr Yves Congar, OP; Fr Eric Doyle, OFM; Fr Pierre Duprey, WF, Under Secretary, Secretariat for Promoting Christian Unity; Revd John Hotchkin, United States Bishops' Ecumenical Commission who was co-chairman and Mgr William Purdy, Secretariat for Promoting Christian Unity, who also acted as co-secretary. These were the terms of reference the Joint Consultation was asked to consider: 'To what extent and in what ways churches with women priests and churches without women priests can be reconciled in sacra- mental fellowship.'[17]

In November 1976, therefore after the publication of the Declaration which had taken place in October, the Plenary Session of the Vatican Secretariat for Promoting Christian Unity accepted the proposal to hold a Joint Consultation which had been made in Rome in November 1975. And in May 1977 the Standing Committee of the Anglican Consultative Council also agreed to the proposed Joint Consultation. On both sides it was understood that the authority of the findings of the Consultation would be only that of its members. The Consul- tation was a service of advice to the two Churches.

We discussed the terms of reference at great length and it was then, as it remains now, a sign of hope that the question was raised at all. The outcome of our deliberations was a short document of eight paragraphs.

This document had a rather strange subsequent history. It was not published by the Vatican Secretariat, but it was submitted in printed form to the Lambeth Conference in August 1978. It should be recalled that the document has no more authority than that of the members of the Consultation who produced it.[18] Bishop Cahal Daly, who represented the Roman Catholic Church at the Lambeth Conference, reasserted the Roman Catholic Church's opposition to the ordination of women. He expressed the anxiety of the Vatican Secretariat about what seemed a prevailing tendency to regard the Roman Catholic Church's position on the ordination of women to the priesthood as unclear and somehow provisional. He stressed that the chief purpose of his statement was to say to the members of the Lambeth Conference that it is not possible to call in question the seriousness and firmness of the Catholic position in this matter. There is no doubt that Bishop Daly had in mind the document produced by the Joint Consultation in Versailles in 1978.

It should be added that Bishop Daly went on to say:

> . . . the Secretariat for the Union of Christians, of which I am a member, would in no way wish to dissociate itself from the hopefulness and the commitment to continued search for reconciliation which was clearly apparent in the Holy Father's letters and has characterized Anglican–Roman Catholic confrontation of this 'new and grave obstacle'.[19]

Therefore if we are to continue the search for reconciliation we will have to go on examining the subject about the ordination of women to the priesthood and remain all of us, Anglicans and Roman Catholics, open to what the Spirit may be saying to the Churches. And as has been said, and must with respect and in truth be repeated, the Declaration, due to its technical character, does not forbid further discussion about the ordination of women.

For these reasons we may enter into dialogue with the

Declaration in regard to the cogency of the arguments it presents for the position it adopts. In a spirit of dialogue I have examined the argument against the ordination of women which the Declaration derives from a particular interpretation of the phrase *in persona Christi*. The fact that women who baptize and marry act *in persona Christi* considerably weakens the Declaration's argument.[20]

In the same spirit I would like to make some comments about the argument from tradition. The Declaration states:

> The Church's tradition in the matter has thus been so firm in the course of the centuries that the Magisterium has not felt the need to intervene in order to formulate a principle which was not attacked, or to defend a law which was not challenged.[21]

Thus the argument is: To ordain a woman would be contrary to the tradition of the Church. In the sense that women have never been ordained to the ministerial priesthood on the Church's authority, this statement stands. It seems, however, more accurate to say: To ordain a woman would be contrary to the practice of the Church. This is no verbal quibble, but an important distinction because the word *tradition* carries far greater weight and authority than does the word *practice*. It is noteworthy that the Declaration, after mentioning the Fathers and the Scholastics, says: 'Since that period and up to our own time, it can be said that the question has not been raised again, for the practice has enjoyed peaceful and universal acceptance.'[22] 'Practice' seems by far the more preferable. To justify the use of the word *tradition* would require a greater number of early witnesses explicitly against the ordination of women, a more cogent argument than 'peaceful and universal acceptance', a more compelling case than silence and less evidence of a negative theology of womanhood. The only argument of any of the Scholastics against the ordination of women that is worthy of serious consideration is one given by Duns Scotus. He maintains that the necessity of maleness for the priesthood is derived from the will of Christ. He argues that the Church would never have presumed on its own authority to deprive the entire female sex of participating in the sacrament of orders.[23] I do not say that this is a convincing argument, but it does have some dignity. In any case, I would be inclined to agree with Begley and Armbuster: 'It is historically more accurate to speak of a non-tradition concerning the ordination of women rather than a tradition against it.'[24]

I came upon a fascinating detail recently from the life of St Thérèse of Lisieux.[25] Among the testimonies from the process of her beatification there is a long and detailed statement by her sister, Céline Martin, whose name in religion was Sister Genevieve of St Teresa. She gave her testimony from 14 to 28 September 1910 before a diocesan tribunal, set up by the Bishop of Bayeux and Lisieux. Sister Genevieve bore witness under oath that:

> In 1897, but before she was really ill, Sister Thérèse told me she expected to die that year. Here is the reason she gave me for this in June. When she realised that she had pulmonary tuberculosis, she said: 'You see, God is going to take me at an age when I would not have had the time to become a priest . . . If I could have been a priest, I would have been ordained at these June ordinations. So, what did God do? So that I would not be disappointed, he let me be sick: in that way I couldn't have been there, and I would die before I could exercise my ministry.' The sacrifice of not being able to be a priest was something she always felt deeply. During her illness, whenever we were cutting her hair she would ask for a tonsure, and then joyfully feel it with her hand. But her regret did not find its expression merely in such trifles; it was caused by a real love of God, and inspired high hopes in her. The thought that St Barbara had brought communion to St Stanislas Kostka thrilled her. 'Why must I be a virgin, and not an angel or a priest?' she said. 'Oh! what wonders we shall see in heaven! I have a feeling that those who desired to be priests on earth will be able to share in the honour of the priesthood in heaven.'[26]

St Thérèse was twenty-four on 2 January 1897, the canonical age for ordination to the priesthood in the Roman Catholic Church at that time.[27] She died on 30 September that same year. This remarkable passage provides much food for thought. One wonders what reaction it provoked in the Promoter of the Faith (known popularly as the 'Devil's Advocate') in Rome as he sifted and examined the evidence for St Thérèse's heroic sanctity. It evidently proved no barrier to her can-onization.

I would like to make one final point. This question ought not to be divorced from the theology of God and the feminine. The mystics and the mystic theologians have much to teach us here. Without embarrassment and with complete confidence so many of them spoke beautifully of God in feminine terms. That has so much relevance to the question about the ordination of women. Let St Anselm, then, have the last word: 'Surely, Jesus, good Lord, you are a mother? Are you not a mother who, like a hen, gathers her chicks under her wings? Indeed, Lord, you are a mother.'[28]

Notes

1. *Declaration on the Question of the Admission of Women to the Ministerial Priesthood* (Vatican City, 1976, published by the Catholic Truth Society, London 1976), p. 5.

2. *Dogmatic Constitution on the Church of Christ* of Vatican I, session IV, ch. 2: 'ideoque eiusmodi Romani Pontificis definitiones ex sese, non autem ex consensu Ecclesiae, irreformabiles esse'.

3. *Did Christ Rule out Women Priests?* (Great Wakering, 1977), pp. 7-8.

4. ibid, p. 8; see *Acta Apostolicae Sedis* 40 (1948), p. 46.

5. *Did Christ Rule out Women Priests?*, p. 8.

6. F.A. Sullivan, SJ, *De Ecclesia I: Quaestiones Theologiae Fundamentalis* (Romae, 1963), p. 355; 'His decretis [Congregationis S. Officii] quae formaliter respiciunt securitatem doctrinae, videntur aequiperandae responsiones Commissionis Pontificalis de Re Biblica.'

7. A. Tanquerey, *Synopsis Theologiae Dogmaticae Fundamentalis* (Parisiis, Tornaci, Romae, 1949), pp. 638-9: 'Assensus religiosus internus his praeberi decretis . . . omnino inferior est assensui fidei tum divinae, tum ecclesiasticae; nec est absolute certus aut omnem erroris possibilitatem excludens, quia circa magisterii declarationes non infallibiles versatur'; see also M. Nicolau, SJ - I. Salaverri, SJ, *Sacrae Theologiae Summa I. Theologia Fundamentalis* (Matriti, 1958), p. 722.

8. *Theological Investigations*, VIII: *Further Theology of the Spiritual Life, 2* (London/New York, 1971), p. 82. This chapter was delivered as an address at the Convention of the Union of German Catholic Women, in June 1964.

9. See *Concilium* 115 (5/1978): J.-P. Jossua and J.B. Metz (eds.), *Fundamental Theology, Doing Theology in New Places*, New York, 1979.

10. *The Shape of the Church to Come* (London, 1974), pp. 113-14.

11. *Theological Investigations*, VIII, p. 82.

12. 'Est-il légitime de consacrer des femmes au ministère pastoral?' in *Verbum caro*, 65 (1963), pp. 5-28.

13. *Theological Investigations*, XX: *Concern for the Church* (London, 1981), pp. 37, 45.

14. 'Ministry Today: Problems and Prospects' in *Worship*, 48 (1974), p. 337.

15. p. 4.

16. *Acta Apostolicae Sedis*, 68 (1976), pp. 599-600.

17. In November 1975 an informal meeting took place in Rome of Anglicans and Roman Catholics at the Vatican Secretariat for Promoting Christian Unity. It recommended in a Note to the Archbishop of Canterbury and Cardinal Willebrands these precise terms of reference; see *Anglican-Roman Catholic Consultation on the Ordination of Women to the Priesthood*, p. 3.

18. The text of the document was published in *The Tablet* (5 August 1978), pp. 762-3.

19. See *The Tablet* (5 August 1978), p. 762.

20. Eric Doyle, OFM, 'The Question of Women Priests and the Argument *in persona Christi*' in the forthcoming issue of the *Irish Theological Quarterly*.

21. p. 6.

22. p. 6.

23. *Lib. IV Sent.* d.25, q.2, 4 in *Joannis Duns Scoti . . . Opera Omnia* XIX (Parisiis, 1894 (Vivès)), p. 140a. Scotus also presents other familiar and now unconvincing arguments. He states that a woman cannot receive orders because at least since the Fall a woman is not permitted to hold any position over men; see ibid., p. 140b.

24. John J. Begley, SJ - Carl J. Armbuster, SJ, 'Women and Office in the Church' in *The American Ecclesiastical Review*, 165 (1971), p. 97.

25. This was drawn to my attention by Miss Ann Marie Stuart of Canterbury, a former student of mine. I wish to express my thanks to her for this reference.

26. *St Thérèse of Lisieux by those who knew her: Testimonies from the process of beatification*, ed. and trans. by C. O'Mahony, OCD (Dublin, 1975), pp. 155-6.

27. This has been altered in the new Code of Canon Law which came into effect on 27 November 1983; see Canon 1031, par. 1: 'The priesthood

may be conferred only upon those who have completed their twenty-fifth year of age . . .'

28. *S. Anselmi Cantuariensis Archiepiscopi Opera Omnia*, vol. III . . . Ad fidem codicum recensuit Franciscus Salesius Schmitt, OSB, Edinburgi MDCCCCXLVI, *Oratio 10*, pp. 40-1.

THREE

Women and Authority in the Scriptures*

George Carey

Following an address about the ministry of women, I fell into conversation with two young women students who were at one and the same time encouraged and troubled by what they had heard. 'I agree that women are not treated as equals in the Church', said one, 'but the Bible seems to say that God has given authority to men'. 'Yes', added the other, 'the problem appears to be that if one takes the Bible seriously and honestly we must come to the reluctant conclusion there is a sexual hierarchy in the Bible. The place of women is in the pew not in the pulpit, at the altar rail, not at the altar. It's hard – but that is how it is.'

But is it? Does the New Testament, in fact, impose a binding restriction on the ministry of women, forbidding them to participate in the leadership of the church?

There are two separate approaches we must take to answer this question. First, we have to ask what is God's plan for human destiny and, second, we must consider the testimony of the verses in the Pauline writings which appear to limit the exercise of the ministry of women. It is important to start with our theology of humanity because otherwise the texts which confused the two students mentioned will appear to be a giant obstacle to the ordination of women.

Whatever our views are concerning the interpretation of Genesis 1—3 it is commonly agreed that the passage is theologically important for our concept of humanity. 'Let us

* First published as a pamphlet by the Movement for the Ordination of Women

make man [Adam] in our image, after our likeness; . . . So God created man in his own image, in the image of God he created him; male [Zakar] and female [Negebhah] he created them' (Genesis 1.26-7). This is a striking passage not only because humanity is seen as the crown and climax of God's creation but also because it is viewed as two sexes sharing the generic name, Adam. Both are made in the image of God. The emphasis upon equality and complementarity is struck at the very beginning. Roger Beckwith, an Evangelical theologian hostile to the ordination of women has to admit: "There is an emphasis here on the equality of male and female and on their unity, both in relation to God and in relation to the lower creation."[1] Beckwith acknowledges that the parallel passage in chapter 2 reinforces the earlier teaching of the unity and equality of the two sexes. Thus, a very important theological principle emerges from the two chapters - that male and female are viewed as complementary creatures who together are made in the image of God. Together they are the crown of creation and they need each other to survive.

The description of the Fall shows that sin has altered that relationship and made it abnormal in God's sight. We cannot concern ourselves here with the meaning of the Fall; for our purposes we note that God's sentence takes two forms. For both of them it is exclusion from God's presence and they are alone in a creation which is now alien to them. But for man it also includes labour and for women their domination by man. 'Your desire shall be for your husband and he shall rule over you.' The author is making the point that the Fall introduced a serious change in the relationship between men and women. The unity and equality expressed so clearly in chapter 1 is replaced by the authority of one over the other. Sin has spoiled not only the spiritual relationship between creator and creature but has also affected the social relationships between men and women.

Now, to what extent is this affected by the coming of Christ? Does his message have anything to say directly about social relationships now - or are we forced to admit that the doctrine of the new creation is irrelevant to such issues? We must look at the bearing of the New Testament on this issue.

It is noteworthy that women have a prominent place in the ministry of Jesus. The freedom with which Jesus moved among women has no parallel among his rabbinic peers in first-century Judaism. He affirmed them as people, he accepted ministry from them. He spent a great deal of time in their company. They were witnesses of his death and, more significantly, of his resurrection. Now from this we cannot deduce that it follows automatically that divine authority is given to women to officiate on the same basis as men. But it does indicate that with Jesus a different spirit and attitude prevailed towards women. They may not be included among the Twelve - but neither for that matter were non-Jews - but they were among the close circle of his intimate friends. The cultural and social barriers of his day would have made it impossible for him to take the unprecedented step of appointing them as apostles even if he had desired to. Speculating apart, it is clear that Jesus affirms the personhood and dignity of women and opens for them a new status in the Kingdom of God.

It is important also to realize the significance of the achievements of Christ for his people. The excitement and joy of the first Christians shines through the New Testament. They were only too well aware that Christianity was not 'pie in the sky when I die' - it was certainly that, but much more besides. Christ had opened the way to the Father, abrogated the Old Testament priesthood and as priest and victim had reconciled mankind to God. He had made 'peace through the blood of the cross' and created a new people for his glory. As a consequence all social, sexual, religious and cultural barriers are swept away. This, of course, is the theological significance of baptism - all are welcome to join the Christian family. Unlike Judaism which had no initiatory rite for women comparable to circumcision for men, baptism was for all. Baptism signifies that we are joint heirs. Paul enunciates this theology in that splendid passage in Galatians 3.26-8:

> For in Christ Jesus you are all sons of God, through faith. For as many of you as were baptized into Christ have put on Christ. There is neither Jew nor Greek, there is neither slave nor free, there is neither male nor female; for you are all one in Christ Jesus.

Now it is contended by some that the passage says nothing about social relations, still less about ministry in the Church. It is simply saying that salvation is not restricted to any one class. It is universal and available to all. So Roger Beckwith argues:

> The context is one of salvation - more precisely, of sonship, faith, union with Christ, baptism, and inheritance of the promises of Abraham. For these blessings, Jew and Gentile, slave and free, male and female are alike eligible. All alike can be saved, all alike can be baptised without distinction. But whether there are other distinctions between Jew and Gentile, slave and free, male and female, which still remain, the passage neither says nor implies.[2]

But can we limit the passage to its spiritual interpretation? Take the first category - Jew and Greek. The first major division in the early Church was precisely about relationships between Jewish and Gentile Christians. The New Testament rams home the point in the Acts of the Apostles and in Galatians that the gospel affects the way we live, the food we eat and the way we worship. Beckwith's contention that the context is merely that of salvation is sheer expediency; the verse comes at the climax of Paul's argument against those who wanted to make social divisions between Jewish Christians and Gentile Christians.

Then the second category is significant too - slaves and free. How easy it would have been in a different age to have opposed the emancipation of slaves on the ground that the verse says nothing about the status of the slave in society. Indeed, it could be argued, it is the spiritual that Paul is concerned about. What a superficial understanding of the text that would be! Because in essence it says everything about slavery, that if a slave is accepted by Christ, he is accepted by Christians and the edifice of human bondage begins to crack.

Is it possible, then, that we can limit Paul's phrase 'male and female' purely to a spiritual relationship? Surely not. In Christ there is a new creation; we are accepted in him as brothers and sisters, and our sexual natures are no longer barriers to him and to us. Scripture does not say that he became male but that he was made man to redeem mankind and to create a new humanity which has social as well as spiritual implications. To say then to a woman: 'I'm sorry but Paul's words do not have any bearing upon social relationships, your status as a Christian alongside men, the use of your gifts in church . . .' is to make a mockery of this teaching; it is to remove the heart from the Christian faith and make it a filleted faith. It is furthermore a cruel blow to a woman who, rightly, sees the verse as pointing beyond the restrictions which culture and history have imposed.

I think it is very likely that Paul himself did not see the full implications of this lofty teaching that he was giving. It is the nature of Scripture, after all, that under the Holy Spirit new insights and fresh understandings are discovered in different generations. We must not attribute omniscience to Paul. He lived within the limitations of his own culture and he could not have known the total implications of the Christian concept of humanity. As we have already observed, his views about slavery were not exactly developed and neither were his views about the Christian attitude to the state (Romans 13.1). Nevertheless, his teaching about discipleship, baptism, the new creation, and the dignity of humanity in God's sight, form a revolutionary basis for human relationships.

Pentecost from one perspective is not only the birthday of the Christian Church, it is its baptism as well. On that day the Church received the baptism of the Holy Spirit. Thereafter every individual Christian participates in this baptism and all are made members of the family of God. There is no evidence that the Spirit came upon men only - indeed Peter quotes Joel to show that at the coming of the Messiah all will share in the gift of the Spirit (Acts 2). Thus we see in the early Church men and women working together in the fellowship and using their gifts in God's service. Women exercise gifts of leadership, if Priscilla is anything to go by (Acts 18.1, see also, Romans 16.1); their homes become the meeting places for Christians, and no doubt as hosts they would have played important roles in the community (Acts 16.15); they engage in many forms of Christian service and also in the diaconate (Romans 16.1,

Philippians 4.2). The numerous mentions Paul makes of women indicate their importance in his churches (Romans 16, Colossians 4.15). They are given the gift of prophecy (Acts 21.9) and thus take a part in the second great order of ministry mentioned frequently in the New Testament - apostles, prophets and teachers (1 Corinthians 12.28). Calvin's comment that the daughters of Philip only prophesied 'at home or in a private place outside the common assembly' is a feeble fatuous apology of an argument. It is quite apparent from 1 Corinthians 11.5 that women did exercise the gift of prophecy in the congregation.[3]

Pentecost adds therefore a new dimension to the question of ministry in the church. Over against controls imposed by society and culture a new theology comes into being inspired by the notion that the gifts the Spirit gives should be used for the good of the people of God. The analogy that Paul uses is that of a human body. Just as a body is composed of many different organs and parts and each has its proper function, so it is with the church, the Body of Christ. If the spirit is the originator of the gift, it must be employed for the benefit of the body. (1 Corinthians 12.13ff).

This theology therefore asks a number of pertinent questions about the Christian ministry. If the Spirit of God is bestowed on all the Church, what right has the Church got to suppress genuine gifts of the Spirit? If indeed the Church refuses to allow the gifts solely on the basis that they are being exercised by 'slaves or gentiles or women', would not that constitute a refusal to accept the significance of Pentecost for an out-working of a theology of the Church and ministry?

I now turn to a group of texts which appear to point away from the exciting theology of humanity above. Five restrictions are imposed upon women: they must cover their heads (1 Corinthians 11); they must keep silent in the congregation (1 Corinthians 14.34); they must not lead in prayer (1 Timothy 2.8ff); they must not teach and they must not exercise authority over men (1 Timothy 2.12).

We cannot avoid the fact that these verses present an

uncomfortable challenge to all of us who see Scripture as
conveying God's word to us. Do we then have to admit that the
New Testament is set implacably against the full exercise of
women's ministry? Do we indeed find in these writings a kind
of permanent 'canon law' which limits the role of women in the
Church for all time?

1 Corinthians is a response to a letter sent to St Paul
from Corinth. It is very likely that in chapter 11 Paul is
answering a question about the relation between men and
women especially in public worship. C.K. Barrett conjectures
whether the inquiry was about 'the necessity to observe
conventional distinctions in a community in which there were
no longer male and female' (Galatians 3.28).[4] Whatever the
background, Paul does not deny the ministry of women in the
church as prophets (1 Corinthians 11.5) but he insists that
Christian women should not break the custom of wearing a veil
in public. He argues:

> But I wish you to know that Christ is the head of every man, the
> man is head of the woman, and God is the head of Christ . . . for a
> man ought not to veil his head for he is the image and glory of God,
> but woman is the glory of man. For man did not come from woman
> first but woman from man . . .

Roger Beckwith argues from this passage that a woman 'will
not behave herself immodestly in the congregation in any
respect, which certainly means that she will not undertake
offices of authority over men. But note that there is nothing
degrading in this subordination . . . because Christ is subordinate to God and there is nothing degrading in the internal
relations of the Holy Trinity.'[5] Beckwith's argument is
extraordinarily superficial in a number of respects.

First, the passage does not say anything about offices in the
church. Paul is talking about what a woman wears in the
congregation. Paul obviously accepts without qualm the fact
that women are active in the congregation. C.K. Barrett
contends in his commentary that 1 Corinthians 11.5 is meaningless unless women were moved to pray and prophesy aloud in
the Christian congregation. 'Paul assumes that women will
offer public prayer and utter the kind of public speech known as

prophecy, and he simply regulates the way they do this.'[6]

Secondly, if Paul is attempting to produce a model of male-female relations based upon the Godhead, the argument can backfire seriously. The progression is - God over Christ, Christ over man, man over woman. If Roger Beckwith is correct that the analogy is drawn from the Holy Trinity, the word 'subordination' is scarcely fitting. Indeed the mutual relations of the Godhead rule out the kind of subordination he is arguing for. If the paradigm for ministry were the Trinity there would be free and unrestrictive exercise of the gifts of women in ministry! No, it is invalid to read back the Trinity into this passage. Paul's argument, if pressed too far, would suggest a subordinationist christology untypical of his theology generally. Third, it is significant and interesting that his argument that women are not made directly in the image of God but in the image of man, is drawn not from Genesis 1 but from a rabbinic understanding of Genesis 2. Surely we would not want to say that Paul's definitive thinking concerning the 'image of God' is found in this passage? Barrett comments that 'Paul might have reached a different conclusion if he had started from Genesis 1.27'.[7] Finally, we observe that this passage which seems to put women firmly in their place ends in a surprising affirmation of the interdependence of men and women (1 Corinthians 11.11-12).

What is therefore very clear from the passage is the way culture and Paul's rabbinic background influence the issue of men-women relationships in the congregation.

We seem to be confronted with a further problem when 1 Corinthians 14.35 is considered. In this passage Paul urges women to keep silent in the church. Of course it may be referring to women chattering and disturbing the worship in an unseemly way. If however it is barring women from ministering to the congregation it is a direct contradiction of 11.5 where Paul refers to the ministry of women prophets. He had ample opportunity to condemn the practice earlier but did not. Why not? Barrett considers two possibilities. Either that this verse was not Pauline but was added as a gloss later or that, because of their chatter, Paul commands women to be silent in the interests of good order. The latter seems to be the better of the two hypotheses, because it avoids the necessity to accuse Paul of self-contradiction or to go to the lengths of seeing verse 35 as an interpolation.

1 Corinthians, together with many of Paul's epistles, gives us glimpses of the early Church attempting to relate their understanding of the gospel to the social conditions of their own day. As that gospel made inroads into the Church's understanding of social relationships apparent contradictions and uneasy compromises were bound to occur. 1 Corinthians allows us to see the tension between Spirit and church order.

If then we find in 1 Corinthians tension between Paul's doctrine of the Church under the Spirit and his expectation about the conduct of worship in Corinth, we find in the Pastorals a more rigid attitude still concerning women. It is not at all certain that Paul wrote the Pastorals, although many are inclined to agree that Pauline fragments are embedded in the letters. Whether he wrote them or not they are still Scripture to us and deserve careful attention. According to the Pastorals there is now a more developed church life: the word 'bishop' occurs only in the singular, whereas 'elders' and 'deacons' are mentioned in the plural. Careful instructions are laid down for the choosing of church leaders, but of women leaders there is no trace. Instead women are told to hold their tongue and on no account to take leadership or to speak in church.

Taken absolutely on its own, the teaching of the Pastorals appears to give little room for manoeuvre. It simply will not do to accept Beckwith's interpretation that 'the Pastorals teach that women must not teach or exercise authority, at any rate in mixed congregations'.[8] If we take 1 Timothy 2.12 as it stands, it goes further than Beckwith allows - it forbids women to teach, full stop! This would have disastrous consequences upon the modern Church and, indeed, the missionary movement, if we applied such a text woodenly.[9] We must note that the practice of the Jewish synagogue provides the background. The writer is addressing the needs of his own people in his own time. What we have to ask is: To what extent do instructions about first-century order apply to us today?

When interpreting difficult passages of scripture, two important principles need to be applied. First, we must ask how do the texts relate to the general teaching of scripture? We have already noted that 1 Corinthians 11 could suggest that Paul held a subordinationist christology if we separated the passage from the rest of his theology. Likewise, in the case of the 'hard' sayings about women's ministry, we find them going against the general tenor of such doctrines as the priesthood of all believers, the doctrine of baptism, the gifts of the Spirit, the status of women before God. As we have seen it is dangerous to over-spiritualize these doctrines – either they relate to the whole of life or not at all.

Secondly, to what extent are the verses in question culturally conditioned? There are two ways in which culture may influence the prophetic message of the gospel. First it may blunt the message. An illustration of this in the New Testament is the way slavery is tackled. Because they were children of their time the New Testament writers did not express directly the gospel's challenge to slavery. The challenge is there, in the doctrine of baptism and the command to love but it was eighteen hundred years before the Church saw clearly the implications of the gospel upon the institution of slavery. Secondly, culture may obscure the message of the gospel so that we end up embracing the culture of the first century – imagining it to be the gospel for us today. I think it is all too easy to take Paul's teaching about the position of women in this way and assume that it is self-evident that we must take it as God's Word for us now as it was when it was first written. In a helpful article, James Dunn points to the element of cultural relativity in the New Testament: 'We should accept that there will be texts which cannot function for us as Word of God in the sense in which they were written (because of their covenant conditionedness or culture conditionedness, or both).' He goes on to say that we can accept them as God's Word in their historical setting but that it may be the case that they are not God's Word for us now. He appeals for an interaction of a strictly historical exegesis with a prophetic openness to the Spirit which he believes to be the basis for a truly scriptural hermeneutic.[10]

It is important to bear in mind Professor Dunn's remarks and to maintain a proper balance between the finality of the Christian revelation as contained in Scripture and its openness to new possibilities in Christ. On the one hand, Scripture is the witness to God's saving revelation in Christ and 'contains all things necessary for salvation'. But, on the other hand, the application of the great biblical truths requires time to recognize and work out and vary according to circumstance. So, to the question, why is it that it is only in this century that the issue of women's ministry has become such a burning problem, we have to reply that it is only recently that full educational opportunities and political and sexual freedom has made the question possible. It is a blot upon the Christian tradition that, once again, the running has been made by secular society. We have been slow to recognize the biblical testimony to the complementarity of men and women in Christian anthropology and we have been reluctant to allow the Spirit's gifts to flow through women.

As we have acknowledged readily, it is impossible to give full and undisputed scriptural proof for the right of women to take their place alongside men in the Church. For that matter I wonder how many doctrines we take for granted have a clear undisputed base in Scripture? One of the basic reasons for the unclarity about the place of women's ministry in the Church is simply that the New Testament was not addressing itself to our situation and we cannot go to it expecting to find clear instructions concerning church order today - anymore than we can find clear guidance about abortion and genetic engineering. What we do find however, is a description of redeemed humanity which binds men and women together in Christ and which gives a new status and openness to their natures.

Notes

1. Roger Beckwith, 'The Bearing of Holy Scripture', in P. Moore (ed.), *Man, Woman, Priesthood* (SPCK, 1978), p. 47.

2. op. cit., p. 56.

3. Cited in Paul K. Jewett, *The Ordination of Women* (Grand Rapids, W. Eerdmans, 1980), p. 65.

4. C.K. Barrett, *The First Epistle to the Corinthians*, New Testament Commentaries (A. & C. Black, 1968), p. 347.

5. Beckwith, op. cit., p. 50.

6. Barrett, op. cit., p. 250.

7. ibid., p. 248.

8. Beckwith, op. cit., p. 55.

9. In an interesting private note Dr Jim Hickinbotham, former Principal of St John's College, Durham, and Wycliffe Hall, Oxford, writes: 'If it is theologically wrong for women to bear authority in the Church, it must be equally wrong for them to do so in society - and anyone who for this reason rejects women bishops must hold it to be un-Christian to allow a woman to be Queen or Prime Minister or to hold positions in the professions or commerce and industry. Also, of course, women must be ejected from all our synods!'

10. James Dunn, 'The Authority of Scripture according to Scripture' (*The Churchman*, vol. 96, no. 3, 1982-3), pp. 215-22.

FOUR

'The Faltering Words of Men': Exclusive Language in the Liturgy

Janet Morley

'Christians are formed by the way in which they pray, and the way they choose to pray expresses what they are.'
'Words, even agreed words, are only the beginning of worship. Those who use them do well to recognise their transience and imperfection.'

(Preface, ASB)[1]

Major liturgical documents, it seems, are always published in an atmosphere of heated debate, and their prefaces reflect this. The Book of Common Prayer eclipses most modern efforts, in its forthright and robust approach to opponents. These are frankly referred to as 'factious, peevish and perverse spirits' who cannot 'be satisfied with any thing that can be done in this kind by any other than themselves'.[2] The tone of the preface to *The Alternative Service Book 1980* is much more tactful, but it is carefully worded to reply to implicit opposition; its comments about cultural specificity, liturgical pluralism, and the essential imperfection of all religious language clearly reveal that there are those who believe the Book of Common Prayer to be a thoroughly adequate expression of the Church's unity, phrased in language of 'timeless qualities'. The preface refers to the existence of a 'detailed public debate', and the deeply felt sense of disquiet about the whole project is reflected in the direct offer of reassurance to those who fear that new forms of worship might 'erode the historical foundations of the Church's faith' (ASB, p. 10).

Why do proposals for change in the use of liturgical language arouse such anxiety? I believe the response has to do with the paradoxical nature of language itself - a paradox that is perhaps particularly evident in religious discourse. For, as the initial quotations from the ASB preface suggest, words are both remarkably powerful and fundamentally inadequate. And they are so in ways quite different from what an unselfconscious 'common sense' view of language might propose. One might expect that language is 'powerful' when it succeeds in describing reality with great accuracy, and 'inadequate' when it fails to do so. Again, one might suppose language to be merely a tool of human thought: that people choose to use this or that expression according to its fitness for the occasion, and depending on how much they care about correct usage. In either case, language is regarded as the icing on the cake of reality, a sort of pale reflection, in words, of what is solidly 'there' to be described.

However, it is arguable – and the editors of the ASB clearly would so argue – that language fails us precisely where we would expect to rely on it, while it exerts a sinister power exactly when we regard it as well under our control. The quotation about the 'transience and imperfection' of words is not, I think, an expression of Christian humility on the part of the authors, nor indeed an attempt to forestall criticism of their document. Instead, it proposes that words do not in fact *describe* reality, especially the reality of God, in any direct way at all; all language is metaphorical, and to cling to any formulations as unproblematical statements about 'reality' is actually dangerous. At the same time, it is suggested, we need to recognize the enormous capacity words have to construct the way in which we think about ourselves and our faith:

Christians are formed by the way in which they pray. (ASB, p. 10)

If liturgical reform, then, means that we are not just exchanging one bag of tools for another, but attempting a painful exchange of identity, and if, moreover, it involves letting go of our accustomed reliance on the adequacy of words to mirror reality, it is not surprising that there is considerable resistance to change – hence the fervent debate.

There is, however, one area of current concern about language which is startling in its absence from either the preface or the text of a document published as recently as 1980, and that is the debate about 'sexist' or (the term I prefer) 'exclusive' language in church. This is broadly defined as the practice of using generically (with reference to the whole of humanity, or to all Christian believers) terms like 'men', 'brothers', 'sons', 'he' and 'him', which ordinarily denote males, and the overwhelming use of 'masculine' titles, when addressing or referring to God. In the case of the first, argument has centred on whether or not women are felt to be (invisibly) present within 'mankind'; in the second, it is open to debate whether sexuality (but especially female sexuality) is, or should be, included in our concept of God. Current pressure to alter our practice raises those issues about language, to which the ASB is so sensitive, in a particularly emotive form. If we are 'formed' by the way in which we pray together, it is highly significant for women's (and men's) identity, whether those aspects of humanity that have been associated with the 'feminine' are present in our worship or not. And yet the editors of the ASB, with apparent unselfconsciousness, fall into an unfortunate, ironic use of the male generic:

> Only the grace of God can make up what is lacking in the faltering words of men. (p. 11)

Quite.

It is clear that the tone of the debate, in this country at least, has altered very considerably during the past few years. The innocence of the ASB's preface is paralleled by the unhesitating retention of 'man' within the text, both in echoing traditional translations of the creed:

> For us men and for our salvation. (p. 123)

and in modern formulations:

> We have sinned against you and against our fellow men. (p. 120)

There has apparently been no attempt to eliminate the male generic, even when a simple omission would leave the sense untouched; the text is strewn with gratuitous 'men'. Jean Mayland, who served on the commission which produced the

ASB, confirms that the issue was dismissed without debate:

> No one took me seriously when I raised the matter of 'sexist' language. (Letters, *The Times*, 13 Oct. 1983)

But, as she points out, 'only a few years later, the situation is very different'. In July 1983, the editor of *News of Liturgy* (also a member of the ASB commission) comments that the usage 'does start to stand out in the text of prayers now'.

Part of the change in the 'feel' of the debate has been due to altered – or at least challenged – practice in society as a whole. For instance, the gradual decline of the generic connotation of 'man' has been charted in various places, and indeed it was excluded from the most recent edition of *Roget's Thesaurus*. But there have been a number of significant initiatives within the churches. In 1980, as part of its discussion about the overall revising of its hymnbook (a document in Methodism at least as sacred as the Book of Common Prayer), the *Methodist Recorder* invited (and received) debate about 'sexist' language. The continued interest has led the editors of *Hymns and Psalms* actually to emend certain hymn texts, endeavouring 'as far as possible . . . to offer hymnody which takes equal account of the place of both women and men in the life of the church, so that no one may be inhibited by insensitive editing from making a full offering of herself or himself in God's service.'[3]

Some of the most established living hymn-writers, notably Brian Wren and Fred Kaan, have revised their earlier texts to exclude the male generic, and Brian Wren has written a number of hymns using feminine terms for God. This is exceptional, but a scan of general theological writing published in the last few years will establish that an increasing number of authors (by no means all of them self-consciously radical) are avoiding generic 'man', and refer to the Christian or the human being as 'he or she'. A few also omit the male pronoun when referring to God.

Alteration in public worship is fairly advanced in some countries, though not here; at the World Council of Churches Assembly in Vancouver in 1983, the worship was notably inclusive. And it would be true to say that many Canadian and US Christians now experience 'culture shock' when entering the majority of British churches, which are not sensitive to the issue. It is, however, fascinating to observe the interest which the national secular press takes in the issue as occasion arises. I was associated with the British reprinting of a United Church of Canada document *Guidelines for Inclusive Language* (snappily retitled *Bad Language in Church*). It received a wide coverage, including a leader in *The Times*,[4] which raised a number of serious philosophical issues; and I received a hefty postbag, which gave me much thought about the fundamental emotions stirred by the issue. Both of these seem crucial to explore.

A feature of the response to pressure for inclusive language is the paradoxical insistence that, on the one hand, the issue is too trivial to be discussed and, on the other, that to raise it is positively satanic. The charge that those who study language are engaged in 'triviality' is offered by people of many political persuasions; but it is difficult to avoid the suspicion that something important is being denied, because of the hostile tone in which the charge is made and the hasty provision of suggestions for more fruitful ways of spending one's time. The accusation about colluding with the Devil seems to arise out of the belief that the traditional patriarchal relationship between men and women is divinely ordained, that tampering with exclusive language will destroy this; and that the text of Scripture can and must be preserved unaltered till the Day of Judgement or the consequences will be unspeakable. This 'trivial'/'demonic' polarity seems to me to emerge from the painfully equivocal status of language that I described earlier; the struggle is to know how far words are demonically powerful, and to what extent they are utterly irrelevant – are they sacred or meaningless? To be required to become self-conscious about our use of language is inevitably uncomfortable, because it exposes that struggle. In the case of exclusive language, to examine its effects is to reveal another deep dilemma, which it would be far more soothing to leave alone. As one woman put it to me, in some distress: 'I thought I was a member of the human race until the feminists started pointing out to me that I wasn't included in the language.'

To the feminist proposition that language reflects and

reinforces a systematic exclusion of women from our definition of humanity, a number of objections are advanced. A common theme among letters that I received about exclusive language is that the issue matters only to a few unrepresentative and essentially neurotic women, who are flaunting their inferiority complex, whilst unconsciously despising their own sex. Or, as *The Times* rather more delicately put it, 'insult' is perceived only by 'a peculiar type of single-mindedness'.

Even those who are inclined to be sympathetic tend to represent their concern as 'pastoral'. The preface to *Hymns and Psalms* states that: 'textual alterations have been made only where these could be *pastorally* as well as editorially sanctioned' (my emphasis). For me, the term 'pastoral', used in this context, presents problems; for it implies that alterations have been made, not from principle, but in order to avoid offending those who may be particularly sensitive. A 'pastoral' problem is one that is perceived as arising out of the weakness of those few individuals who, for some reason, feel victimized; it does not normally imply a response to the oppression of a group, nor any degree of responsibility for the oppression on the part of those who are urged to be sympathetic. An examination of hymn 237, 'Hills of the North, rejoice', with its counterpart in the old *Methodist Hymn Book* (815) demonstrates the problem. It is clear that this old missionary hymn has been not merely emended, but extensively rewritten, so as to remove its neo-colonial assumptions. I suspect that the editors have described their work as 'pastoral' in an effort to avoid the unwelcome word 'ideological'. But to imply that the rewriting of exclusive language (whether racist or sexist) is not ideological is to limit the issue in a comforting but unhelpful way. It is to suggest that language use has no effect on those who do not feel excluded: it is only a problem when feminists make it so. This is to be unrealistic about the formative power of language, which, as I have suggested, profoundly influences the way we think precisely when it feels most 'natural' and neutral. For even where this shaping power is acknowledged, the temptation to limit the effect of linguistic conventions is very great. Colin Buchanan, in *News of Liturgy* (July 1983), reflecting on the traditional masculine terms for God, addresses only the 'consciousness' of women:

How do men's terms affect their prayers?

The unspoken question about *men's* prayers is, of course, equally fascinating.

Another way in which the far-reaching ideological dimension is denied is through the proposition that the issue is purely a grammatical one. My correspondents have assured me that consulting a dictionary proves that 'there is, of course, no word "sexist"; it means nothing'. What is more, 'man' includes 'woman' because 'anyone with any education at all' knows that it does. There are two interesting assumptions here: first, that dictionaries and grammatical rules are free from ideological bias or rationalization, and second, that the current usage of the male generic is unambiguously clear. There is not space here to chart the etymology of the word 'man' from its genuinely generic origins to its predominantly 'male' con-notations, but it is worth noting that when grammatical rules were formulated, it was common for an ideological justification to be evident. In 1746, John Kirkby published his *88 Grammatical Rules*, of which no. 21 states that the male gender is more 'comprehensive' than the female gender.[5] Here, a contemporarily acceptable precedence has been 'read back' into the older, generic usage. This should warn us that perceptions of what is 'appropriate' usage may be based on other than simple grammatical reasons.

As to whether the use of generic 'man' is straightforward, this seems to be very far from the case. Recent studies suggest that, even in 'clear' contexts, people of a high educational standard do not envisage women when 'man' is used.[6] Why this might be so can perhaps be deduced from present practice. Even the most fervent grammarian would admit that certain usages of the male generic cannot be applied to women. You may theoretically include women in 'man' or 'mankind', but you cannot greet an individual woman as your 'brother in Christ', or acclaim her as a 'man of God'. (I am not even quite sure whether women are intended to be included in the phrase 'men of God'.) Women are, then, perhaps present in plural statements about 'men', but must be picked out as female where they are mentioned separately. In apparently 'correct' usage, many amusing examples can be discovered where reputable authors have produced sentences in which a generic use of 'man' has meandered imperceptiby into the 'male' meaning, e.g. Erich Fromm's classic statement that 'Man's vital interests are life, food, access to females.'[7]

But, in a less stark way, confusion is becoming increasingly common. I mentioned earlier the growing avoidance of the generic male among religious authors. Unfortunately, the avoidance is not entirely consistent, with the result that ideological slips are tending to show. A writer may think of ordinary Christians as 'sons and daughters of God', but then fall into referring to the literary critic or the theologian as 'he'.[8] Or the male generic is dropped with reference to human beings, except in the time-honoured polarity and partnership, 'man and God'. It is rare for writers who do this to point out their fluctuating usage, but sometimes total confusion is avoided until we reach their chapter on sexuality, where comments about 'man and woman' and 'man and God' may follow each other with bewildering speed. One can only remain entirely comfortable with such confusion by going along with what I believe is an unconscious underlying assumption which our language-structure reinforces: namely, that human beings are normatively male, and so it is *unnecessary* to distinguish 'male' from 'generic' usage. And thus, any difficulty that women may have in determining whether they are included in a given expression is a 'minority' (not a human) problem.

To explore this 'minority problem' a little further. It is sometimes suggested that to show a concern about exclusive language is to fret about the peripheral; that it is a matter of the odd pronoun here and there. But in fact, what lies behind these pronouns is a whole 'discourse', a series of deeply rooted assumptions about women as 'other', which cannot easily be exchanged. I shall try briefly to illustrate this discourse by examining the text of the ASB: not that the document is especially sinful in this respect, but simply that, in the words of its preface,

those who seek to know the mind of the Church of England in the last quarter of the twentieth century will find it in this book. (ASB, p. 10)

To start with the list of lesser saints: there are sixty-six men and ten women. It is inherently improbable that one sex should be nearly seven times as saintly as the other. This unequal balance would be startling if the preponderance were the other way; as it is, the list sits comfortably with the ambiguity of the expression 'men of God'. Why are saintly women less remembered, or deemed to be less important? Focusing on how individuals are described, we see an interesting distinction between the men and the women. Women are nearly all defined in terms of their sexuality: men not at all. The celibate Francis of Assisi is just a 'Friar', but Clare is specifically a 'Virgin'. Josephine Butler is a 'Social Reformer, Wife and Mother', while William Wilberforce is simply a 'Social Reformer'. Why is sexual practice and marital status significant in a woman's vocation, and not a man's? There is a further difference: Catherine of Siena, Teresa of Avila, and John of the Cross, all learned spiritual writers, are each described as 'Mystics', but only the man has the distinction of being called a 'Teacher of the Faith'. Why the caution about offering women authoritative status?

Turning to lectionary choices, we find that similarly interesting patterns emerge, concerning what shall be emphasized about women. An example from each of the Testaments will suffice. In Exodus 1.15-21, there is a spirited and vivid story about two Hebrew midwives, who resist the command of Pharaoh to destroy all newborn males. It provides an excellent example of intelligent civil disobedience in the face of oppression and sets the story of Moses' birth in context, But it is explicitly omitted from the set readings when Exodus 1 is due to be read (Monday of Lent 5, year 1; Sixth Sunday before Christmas, year 2). Why? In the New Testament, one of the most well-attested stories is the anointing of Jesus by a woman; each of the gospel writers gives a version of the event. Only Luke describes the woman as a 'sinner', and she anoints Jesus' feet (the humble gesture of a slave). In Mark and Matthew she is unnamed, but performs a sacramental act of prophetic significance, which Jesus picks out for exceptional emphasis; she anoints his head.

> She has done a beautiful thing for me . . . she has anointed my body beforehand for burying. And truly, I say to you, wherever the gospel is preached in the whole world, what she has done will be told in memory of her (Mark 14.6b, 8-9).

It is inconceivable that such a prediction, made to a male disciple, would have been almost ignored by the Church, but many Christians do not know the story of the anointing of Jesus' head. Artistic depictions of the event are extremely rare; tradition prefers to recall the sinful woman's gesture of humility, and the ASB reflects this emphasis. Luke's story of the prostitute has pride of place as a gospel reading at Communion (Pentecost 10). But the story about an authoritative female act, which was to be told wherever the gospel was preached, is set only for Morning Prayer, either as the alternative reading for Palm Sunday (surely seldom chosen in preference to the Entry into Jerusalem), or relegated to the Tuesday of Epiphany 3. What is it precisely that the Church wishes to remember about women?

Whereas female sexuality seems to be acceptable in liturgy where it represents archetypal human sinfulness, it is hard to find an example of women's bodily experience used as a positive image. For instance, where birth imagery (often used graphically in the Bible) is appropriate, as in the lovely prayer of blessing over the water in the baptismal liturgies, too much closeness to the natural experience is avoided. Reference is made to the waters of the Jordan, to the capacity of water to cleanse and revive, to the waters of the Red Sea and the waters of death, but *not* to the waters of birth. It seems that what may not be said about women is as important as what is traditionally emphasized.

But perhaps the most obvious example of a separate discourse for women is provided by the liturgy set for the celebration 'of any saint'. The manner in which the introductory and post-Communion sentences are set out is most revealing. In each case, there are two alternatives 'for women saints' and one 'general'. Clearly, males are to be identified as normal human beings, and do not need a specifically 'masculine' preface, but women have specially feminine ways of being saintly. These appear to correspond to being an excellent housewife or else a faithful virginal spouse of Christ. It is perhaps understandable that the quotations from Proverbs 31 on the virtuous wife are not thought to be acceptable in referring to male saints. But it is astonishing that the image of the virgin espoused to her heavenly Bridegroom is only thought suitable for women. The assumption appears to have been made that imagery concerning women applies only to women, but imagery about men is neutral and human. Women, then, are caught in a paradoxical discourse: on the one hand, we are urged to perceive ourselves as present in the definition of 'man-kind'; but on the other, we are 'placed' as specifically feminine.

What alternative ways of speaking can we discover, which might challenge this discourse? A common objection to alteration in present practice is the 'aesthetic' argument. As the *Times* leader puts it: 'There is something artificial and clumsy about trying to use the English language to make an ideological point.' I hope I have shown that traditional formulations and emphases are not precisely without ideo-logical content or justification, but it is worth examining the charge of 'artificiality' or 'ugliness', with regard to exclusive language. It is often assumed that the only substitute for 'man' is 'person', and particular exception is taken to the perceived ugliness of this word. One of my correspondents rewrote the 23rd Psalm with 'person' for every male referent ('The Person is my Shepherd') to show me how unpleasant was the result. Clearly, there is a need for a thoughtful approach to style, but I wonder if the unease about alternatives owes less to aesthetic considerations than to the discomfort inherent in a politically self-aware use of language? Or to an intuition that something much costlier than style is at stake? Certainly, some of the terms used by those who are worried about altering liturgical language, especially the imagery, suggest that the anxiety is not just a literary one. I have noticed that metaphors suggesting a violent attack on the vulnerable human body abound. The process of finding inclusive terms is seen as liable to 'impoverish', 'purge', 'murder', or even 'disembowel' the language. Significantly, Maurice Wiles proposes that all the

modern qualifications surrounding the metaphor of God as
'Father' make for an 'emasculated' image!⁹

It seems that, just as the publication of a new prayer book
may seem to threaten to 'erode the historical foundations of the
Church's faith', so the introduction of inclusive language in
worship appears to threaten our bodily and sexual identity.
Among my correspondents, it was commonly supposed that
supporters of inclusive language, in defiance of God's creation
of human beings as male and female, were aiming at 'an
amalgamation of the sexes', or, as one writer somewhat
hysterically put it, 'If God had wanted us to be known as
persons, he would have made us all the same, half and half'.

But if there is anxiety about the human terminology, it is as
nothing, compared with the doubts that arise if we speak of
reducing the 'masculine' language about God. And here again
there is a surprising emphasis on the importance of distinctive
sexuality. It is surprising, because the traditional erotic male
metaphors for God, such as Bridegroom, Husband, and Lover
(so popular in the medieval age) are hardly used in public
worship now. Every new prayer, it seems, starts off with the
mandatory, and sexually 'safe', 'Heavenly Father'. But male
sexuality, associated with God, remains important. One of my
correspondents writes: 'I do not want a sexless God'. Even the
editor of *The Times* feels that to remove 'all metaphors with a
gender connotation would be an impoverishment, and a
particular impoverishment in religious liturgy'.

Now, in one sense, this is encouraging, because there is
clearly a strong link made between removing sexually specific
attributions, and a process of 'depersonalizing' God. And it is
true that a good many suggested inclusive terms lack much
more than just masculine associations; for example, 'Creator,
Redeemer, Inspirer,' may be an illuminating reference to God's
loving activity, but it also loses much that is essential in the
Trinitarian formula, including connotations of personhood and
relatedness.

However, there is also something alarming about the
insistence on male sexuality in God. For it is the *maleness* that

is to be retained. As *The Times* makes clear, female sexuality is not even a possible option:

> The available alternatives to 'He' are 'She' and 'It'. The traditional language makes the best of those three choices: one would prefer not to have the Holy Spirit called 'It'.

Reservations are expressed about using female imagery for God. Robin Leaver, in *News of Hymnody*, July 1983, asks 'Are we not on dangerous ground speaking of the Motherhood of God?'

I want to explore a little this concept of 'dangerous ground', with reference to the feminine, for it seems to me that the way in which we speak of human beings, and the images we feel are appropriate to express our understanding of God, are intimately related. If, as I have suggested, maleness is felt to be normative for human beings, then metaphors which convey an aura of masculine sexuality will feel like a neutral way of imputing personhood to God. And if there exists a discourse about women which (both by what is emphasized and in what is not said) depicts them as 'other', as lacking in authority or significance, as the bearers of an archetypal negative sexuality, as variants of humanity rather than as fully representative human beings, then it is entirely likely that we shall perceive femaleness as a demeaning or blasphemous image for God. In fact, there is no other religious metaphor which inspires similar anxiety. There are those who argue that to call God 'Mother' is explicitly to contradict our Lord's teaching about God. But there is no outcry against the multitude of other images not used by Jesus, but employed in our liturgies and hymnodies; the only requirement, it seems, is to avoid a feminine identification. Again and again in considering this issue, I am brought up against the question: *What is this fearful thing that exclusive language is trying to exclude?* For the emotions that 'inclusiveness' arouses suggest that it is indeed fearful, and not trivial at all. I do not believe that the problem is merely due to a self-satisfied male chauvinist belief in the superiority of the male sex. Nor do I think that, by substituting gender-free terms all round, we shall have confronted the underlying problem.

Here, the work of a secular feminist, Susan Griffin, who has made a special study of pornography, is revealing. She writes of the existence of a 'split culture', of our human tendency to 'split off' parts of ourselves which we do not wish to recognize and affirm (e.g. weakness, bodiliness, sexuality) and project them onto an 'other', who then carries them for us. This 'other' will then be at the receiving end of our punishment – punished both for epitomizing the qualities we resist knowing in ourselves, and also for the self-alienation we suffer as a result of denying part of our own reality. This process of 'splitting' and projection is evident in the creation of any enemy or scapegoat of a culture, but it can be seen in a particularly painful way between men and women. The rejection of all that has been called 'feminine' as a central part of human experience is not, I stress, the 'fault' of individual male chauvinists; it is a function of our whole culture (which Christian tradition has often reflected and legitimated). The rejection is built into our language, into the way we speak, and pray, and teach, and think. And the resistance to language-change illustrates the profound fear which such self-violence gives rise to. For as Susan Griffin argues:

> The projection of a denied self onto an enemy never works. And, in fact, not only does it not work, but the enemy is perceived as someone who gets stronger and stronger and stronger, because with every effort to imaginatively diminish and reduce this enemy, the enemy still returns.[10]

This, then, is why women's lives, experience, authority and sexuality must be diminished, resisted, or demeaned; this is why the feminine must not be named in God. For that which has been omitted from language and liturgy feels like 'dangerous ground' indeed. Imaginatively, what has been denied exerts a sinister power, and we dare not take the risk of naming and accepting it. *The Times* claims that 'a special kind of cordon should be erected round religious language'. It is true, the maintenance of the 'split culture' we inherit does require strong 'cordons' of various kinds, among which exclusive language is one of the most crucial. But do we wish to maintain our splits, or to heal them? While we are carefully protecting the traditional exclusion of the 'feminine' within our liturgies, it is not probable that we shall welcome unreservedly the full contribution of actual women within the life of the Church. Nor, until men are relieved of the burden of being the only truly representative human beings, the only 'neutral' image of God, shall we discover the beauty and particularity of the masculine perspective.

I have argued that our liturgical language, including the language we use about God, does not just happen to omit the feminine, but is (unconsciously) constructed over against the feminine. If this is true, then 'inclusive' language, in the sense of neutral, gender-free terms that do not actually exclude women, is not enough. We need to find a language which names women as whole and human, made in the image of God; a language which positively celebrates the 'feminine' we presently fear. And we need to do this, not because some women feel aggrieved, but because the wholeness of our Christian community depends upon it.

Notes

1. *The Alternative Service Book 1980*, pp. 9–11.
2. Preface to The Book of Common Prayer (first published 1662; CUP), p. ix.
3. Preface to *Hymns and Psalms: A Methodist and Ecumenical Hymnbook*, Methodist Publishing House, 1983.
4. *The Times*, 8 October 1983.
5. Quoted in Dale Spender, *Man-Made Language* (Routledge and Kegan Paul, 1980), p. 148.
6. Research quoted in Casey Miller and Kate Swift, *Words and Women*, Penguin, 1976.
7. Quoted in Brian Wren, 'Sexism in Hymn Language', *News of Hymnody*, July 1983.
8. Maurice Wiles, *Faith and the Mystery of God* (SCM, 1982), pp. 24-5.
9. ibid., p. 118.
10. Susan Griffin, 'Split Culture', *Resurgence*, 101, November/December 1983.

FIVE

The Ordination of Women and the 'Maleness' of the Christ*

R.A. Norris, Jr

Objection has been raised to the proposal to ordain women to the presbyterate (or episcopate) on the ground that such a practice is ruled out by the fact that Jesus was a male. The purpose of this paper is to consider this objection, and to suggest that there are good reasons why it need not be taken seriously - and, indeed, that it rests on premises which might well lead to distortion of basic Christian doctrine. Before that is possible, however, the presuppositions on which the objection rests must be identified and stated, so that they can be discussed.

Argument in support of this objection normally rests in the first instance on the contention that a bishop or presbyter 'represents', 'stands for', 'is an *eikon* of', Christ. It is not necessary here to raise the question of what each of these expressions might mean. It is plain that each of them is susceptible to differing interpretations, and it is equally plain that none of them necessarily means exactly the same as the others.[1] Nevertheless the general drift of the argument is plain. The suggestion is that a woman cannot 'represent' or 'stand for' someone who is a male, and hence that a woman is automatically disqualified from ordination.

Stated in this bald fashion, however, the argument is not persuasive. At least in some senses of the word 'represent', it is clear that women can and do represent males, in ecclesiastical as well as secular businesses. Indeed it might be argued with

---

* Reprinted, with minor revisions, from *The Anglican Theological Review*, June 1976.

equal persuasiveness (though the point is gratuitous here) that baptized women can and do in some sense represent Christ. Hence if the argument is to have force, more must be said to explain why, in this particular case, such representation is impossible. What are the premises which make the argument convincing?

Its first essential premise, clearly, is a conviction about the nature of ordained ministry. The argument assumes not merely that the ordained person in some fashion 're-presents' Christ, but more specifically that such representation occurs and can occur only in and through the reproduction in the minister's person of at least one of the natural human characteristics of Jesus – i.e., maleness. Since (obviously) such a characteristic cannot be conferred by the grace of ordination, it follows that ordination must be limited to persons who naturally possess it.

In the second place, however, the argument can be seen to rest on a further assumption about the economy of salvation. For suppose we ask: Why is it that to represent Jesus is of the very essence of ordained ministry? The answer to this question, once it is raised, seems plain. The business of Christian ministry is the proclamation and actualization of God-with-us; and Jesus as the Christ is in his own person God-with-us. Consequently it must simply be said: *ministry represents Christ because he is the redemption it exists to minister.* If this is true, however, and if it is also true that the redemption which Christ is and embodies can only be represented in a male, then a significant consequence seems to follow. It must be the case that it is not merely *as a male*, but at least partly *in virtue of the fact that he is a male*, that Christ is and can be God-with-us.

Thus, finally, the argument we are considering rests, in the last resort, on a christological premise. It appears to assume not merely that Jesus was a male, but that male, as distinct from female, character was and is a *necessary precondition* of Christ's being what he is and doing what he does. In other words, the reality of God-with-us is such that the natural (and necessary) means of its actualization is a male human being.

Before considering these ideas more or less directly, it seems important to make one or two preliminary points in order to focus the issues in this discussion.

First of all, it is crucial to say something about the relation of the argument we are considering to Christian tradition; and what needs to be said can be put in a single sentence. The argument is virtually unprecedented. It does not in fact state any of the traditional grounds on which ordination to presbyterate or episcopate has been denied to women. To accept the argument and its practical consequence, therefore, is not to maintain tradition, but to alter it by altering its meaning. It is to accord a quite new sense to the Church's long-standing refusal to ordain women. This is not only, or even principally, because the idea that a presbyter or bishop somehow 'images' Jesus in a special way is one which arrived rather late on the scene in Christian history. What is genuinely novel in it is the idea that Jesus' maleness is at least one of the crucial things about him which ecclesial priesthoods must image. This novelty, furthermore, does not fall into the category of minor and peripheral products of pious musing. It touches ultimately, as we have seen, upon questions having to do with Christology and with the economy of salvation; and for that reason it demands the most careful and sceptical scrutiny.

But second, such scrutiny cannot proceed simply by the time-honoured method of trying to see what the tradition has to say about this argument. Such a course is ruled out by the very novelty of what is being argued. The fact is that the tradition does not substantively consider the problem we are asked to discuss. To be sure, it may be possible, without resort to the method of *argumentum e silentio*, to show that there are reasons why this argument is not considered or propounded in the historical sources of Christian doctrine; for it may be that the direction which the development of doctrine took is one which by implication excludes emphasis on the maleness of Jesus as a constitutive factor in the redemption which he embodies and the ministry re-presents. Nevertheless, such evidence can only be indirect; and the problem cannot be solved simply by reference to explicit theological precedent.

In the third place, since this is the case, something must be said about the principles on which the problem is to be settled.

What this means, in effect, is that the nature of the question itself must be clarified. It has been suggested, for example, by some proponents of the argument, that the real issue is simply one of fact. Was Jesus a male or was he not? If he was, then no woman can 'image' or represent him. It is conceded that this conclusion may cause scandal; but the scandal, it is said, is a necessary one. It is an aspect of 'the scandal of particularity', a result of the fact that the Infinite, in order to be 'with us', must assume the reality of finite existence. Thus the simple *datum* that Jesus was a male settles the matter. But can this analysis of the issue in fact stand?

Some confusion is occasioned for our discussion by the introduction at this point of the idea of 'the scandal of particularity'. This expression – whose use is rooted ultimately in Kierkegaard's musings on a sentence of Lessing's[2] – is ordinarily employed to suggest that Christian faith is by its very nature a source of offence to both historical and speculative reason. Christianity makes saving knowledge of the universal and ultimate (God) depend upon a person's relation to a particular and contingent historical event. The historically particular, however, is intrinsically opaque (so the argument runs) to reason, since its very nature is to be unique and unrepeatable (*einmalig*), and hence incapable of being captured in the abstract class-concepts which reason must employ. The Christ-event, therefore, occurs only for faith; and what historical reason can find out and say about Jesus is at best an irrelevance and at worst a concealment of the unique and paradoxical 'happening' of God-with-us. In this view, however, the 'maleness' of Jesus, being an abstract characteristic which he shares with approximately half of the human race, can in no way convey or embody his 'particularity'. On the contrary, to know him as an ordinary male is to know only an *incognito* – to know him in a way inconsistent with that in which faith knows him.[3]

It seems then that, in the argument we are considering, the expression 'scandal of particularity' refers not to the Christ-event in its contingent uniqueness, but rather to an established historical description or classification of Jesus: i.e., to the 'fact' that he was a male. What the statement of this fact is intended to make clear is Jesus' likeness to the other members of a certain class, the class of male human beings. The question then becomes that of the significance to be attached to the fact that this (or some other) class-name can appropriately be applied to Jesus.

And that question cannot be side-stepped. For it must be apparent that there are quite a number of facts about Jesus. To be sure, he was male. He also had a certain complexion and a certain stature. He was Jewish. He belonged to a certain economic class. He was of a certain blood-type. Are we then to suppose that each of these characteristics must be 'imaged' in every presbyter or bishop whom the Church ordains? Presumably not. In that case, however, there must be some reason why one (or more) of these characteristics of Jesus is essential in a minister, and the others, not. The mere fact that Jesus was a male settles nothing. The question - to repeat it - is that of the significance of this or that characteristic of Jesus.

Questions of significance, however, must be answered within a specified frame of reference. One must ask, 'Significance *for what?*' And this is the point at which the crucial issue arises. When the Church speaks - in proclamation, in praise, in theology - about Jesus, what in fact is the focal *concern* which defines its interest in him? With reference to what question do statements about Jesus appear as relevant or irrelevant, significant or unimportant? Now the answer to this query seems clear enough. Indeed, by implication at least, it has already been given in this paper. The Church is interested in Jesus *as the Christ* - christologically. It is interested in him as the one in whom the right relation of humanity to God is, by God's initiative, effected. To put the matter simply, the Church, unlike the historian, the would-be portraitist, the biographer, or the psychiatrist, is not interested as such in Jesuology, but in Christology, in Jesus as the bearer of God's salvation. When, therefore, the question of the significance of Jesus' maleness arises, 'significance' means 'importance in and for the salvific work of God in Christ'. To give a reason why the fact that Jesus was a male forbids the ordination of women is to show that the maleness of Jesus is not only something real about him, but something which is strictly constitutive for the fact that he is God-with-us. Is it?

By way of finding an answer to this question, we must first of all ascertain, in a general way, what human characteristics of Jesus are accorded *christological* significance in the classical tradition of Christian theology. By 'human characteristics' here we must, of course, mean primarily natural and not moral characteristics (such as obedience, faith, love, and the like); for clearly maleness is not a moral characteristic.

When the Church Fathers speak of the incarnation of the divine Logos, they speak in terms which emphasize his participation in the general human condition. This is a line of thought whose beginnings are to be sought in the New Testament itself. There the divine Son is said to become 'flesh',[4] or to assume 'the form of a slave',[5] or to taste death 'on behalf of everyone'.[6] Such expressions as these point not to any special natural characteristic of Jesus, but simply to the fact that in him the divine Word accepts the limitations, the weakness, and the suffering which are the common lot of humanity, Jewish and Greek, male and female. The same interest appears in later Christian writers. When Ignatius of Antioch sets out to describe the paradox of the incarnation, he does so in terms which suggest the importance of the divine Word's involvement in human finitude: fleshliness, createdness, birth, death, and suffering.[7] For Justin Martyr - to take another example - the point of the incarnation is conveyed by mention of the divine Word's birth and crucifixion,[8] as well as his death and resurrection[9] - all of which is summed up in the statement that he 'became man' (*anthrōpos*) or 'came among men as man'. Since in both classical and Hellenistic usage, the Greek word *anthrōpos* signifies primarily 'human person' (as opposed to divine beings and lower animals) rather than 'male person' (as opposed to female) - a fact further evidenced by use of the abstract *anthrōpotēs* to mean not 'maleness' but 'humanity' - this language of Justin's is calculated to call attention to the same truth as does that of the New Testament. What is important *christologically* about the humanity of Jesus is not its Jewishness, its maleness, or any other such characteristic, but simply the fact that he was 'like his brethren in every respect'.[10] 'Oportebat enim eum qui inciperet occidere peccatum, et mortis reum redimere hominem, id ipsum fieri quod erat ille, id est hominem'.[11]

In the age of the great christological controversies, the terms *anthrōpos* and *anthrōpotēs* became the normative equivalents of the Johannine 'flesh'.[12] This usage is canonized in the Nicene Symbol where the verb *enanthrōpein* is used in effect to explain the meaning of 'became flesh'. The growing prevalence of this usage gradually (and not indeliberately) excluded the employment of 'body' as the equivalent of 'flesh'; for the latter custom appeared to encourage, if not to require, an Apollinaristic truncation of Jesus' humanity. The Fathers became sure that in speaking of the incarnation one must emphasize both the wholeness and (therefore) the inclusiveness of Jesus' humanity. It was strictly necessary, for the sake of mankind's salvation, that Jesus be integrally the same sort of being as those whom he saves. This is the ultimate implication of Gregory Nazianzen's well known assertion against Apollinarius: *to . . . aproslēpton atherapeuton* – 'What is not assumed is not healed.'[13]

That this principle is indeed enshrined in the use of *anthrōpos* and its cognates to describe the humanity of Jesus is apparent from the way in which these terms are employed by the representatives of the two conflicting christological schools of the fourth and fifth centuries. The Antiochenes, as we are often reminded, emphasized the concreteness and integrity of the Lord's humanity. For them, the incarnation took place in 'a man'. The point of this stress, however, was scarcely to call attention to the maleness of Jesus. Rather the Antiochenes sought to insist on the authentically human character of the struggle with evil through which redemption was wrought, and by this means to show that it is a redemption in which other human beings can share. For the Antiochenes, in short, the reality of the human 'person' of Jesus was necessary as a presupposition of his saving other human persons. For the Alexandrians, on the other hand, the humanity of Jesus was not 'a man', but the complete set of conditions which essentially characterize human existence. In their case, however, as in that of the Antiochenes, emphasis falls on what Jesus has in common with other human beings *as human*. Any other emphasis would appear to confine the significance of his work to one or another exclusive class of human beings, or to some part or aspect of human nature.

Thus we may say quite firmly in summary that the maleness of Jesus is of no *christological* interest in patristic tradition. Furthermore, it is possible to detect in the development of patristic ideas on the subject a logic which suggests why it never occurred to the Fathers to make any more play with Jesus' sex than they did with his race. What the Fathers learned to understand by 'incarnation' was *the likeness of the Word of God in his humanity to all those who are included within the scope of his redemption*. It is this likeness, expressed in the word *anthrōpos*, which for them explains the logic of the Word's becoming flesh. 'For he became human that we might become divine,' said one of them.[14] And presumably this 'we' (and therefore this humanity) includes women. To make of the maleness of Christ a *christological* principle is to qualify or deny the universality of his redemption.

It may be, however, that there is another line along which it can be argued that Jesus' maleness is somehow intrinsic to his character as God-with-us. The Chalcedonian Christology, after all, insists that the 'person' or 'subject' in Jesus is the Word of God himself. And is not the Word of God, the divine Son, to be conceived somehow as male? Might it not be argued that in the last resort the divine Son *could* only be incarnate as a boy?

The first thing which must be said in connection with any argument of this sort is a word of preliminary clarification. It must be stated quite explicitly that what is being touched on here is not so much Christology as that which the Fathers called 'theology', i.e. the doctrine of God as trinity in unity. The assertion of the 'maleness' of the divine Word raises the issue - prominent in the fourth century - of the nature of God in relation to the attributes which human thought and speech ascribe to him. It also raises, as we shall see, the question of the meaning of 'person' in trinitarian discourse.

For it must be asked, in the first place, whether the ascription of male character to the divine Son is intended to single him out in this respect from the other Persons of the Trinity. Is it being suggested, for example, that the Son is male while the Father and the Spirit are not? Or that Father and Son (say) are male, while the Spirit is female (or neuter)? If such a suggestion is being made, then by the canons of orthodox trinitarianism, it must be repudiated on at least two grounds. In the first place, the epithet 'Son' as applied to the Second Person of the Trinity is acknowledged by the Fathers to be a metaphor whose uses are strictly limited. The point, or points, of the metaphor are two: to assert the *likeness* of Son to Father, and to assert that the Son is 'from' the Father rather than 'from' nothing (i.e. 'created'). Beyond this the metaphor was not pushed. Certainly it was not pressed in such a fashion as to ascribe sexual characteristics to the Son. (Ambrose of Milan: 'Vir autem nomen est sexus: sexus autem non utique divinitati sed naturae deputatur humanae.'[15]) In the second place, the developed doctrine of the Trinity insists that the Persons are distinguished from one another solely by their mutual relations.[16] What sets the Son apart from the Father and the Spirit is the fact that he is directly generated from the Father, *and nothing else*. Indeed it is his absolute likeness to the Father in every respect save that of his 'generation' which the use of *homoousios* by upholders of the Nicene faith was calculated to affirm. There is, then, no sexual differentiation among the persons of the Trinity.

Consequently, if the argument is to hold water, it must be intending to assert not that the Son (as distinct from the Father and the Spirit) is male, but that the divine essence or nature, common to the three Persons, is male. To the Church Fathers, however, such a proposition would seem not so much false as absurd. 'What God is in essence and nature, no man ever yet has discovered or can discover.'[17] 'We . . . have learned that his nature cannot be named and is ineffable. We say that every name, whether invented by human custom or handed down by the Scriptures, is indicative of our conceptions of the divine nature, but does not signify what that nature is in itself.'[18] This principle - that of the ineffability or incomprehensibility of the divine nature - was a principal pillar of the orthodox argument against radical Arianism; and what it expresses is not merely the idea of the infinity of the divine essence, but also God's exemption from the categories and contrarieties of the finite world. As a first principle of the Christian understanding of God, it applies *a fortiori* to all epithets which express or imply sexual symbolism, whether masculine or feminine. Male or female imagery[19] may – and indeed, in practice, must – be employed to characterize God's ways of relating himself to humanity in creation and redemption (as, for that matter, may 'neuter' imagery). But to ascribe sexual character to the divine nature is to subject the Infinite *in its own being* to the limitations of the created world, and thus implicitly to substitute an idol for God – to domesticate the Almighty by allowing a tradition of 'iconography' to function as a rule for God's Being.[20]

In the light of these considerations, it must be said that as from a strictly christological, so from a theological, perspective the fact of Jesus' maleness is not, for the classical tradition, a constitutive factor in the meaning of 'God-with-us'. It is definitive neither of what is meant by 'us' in that expression, nor of what is meant by 'God'. So we are left roughly where we were at the end of the last section. Maleness is not constitutive of Jesus as the Christ. On the contrary, Christology envisages him as the representative *human being* – a category which presumably includes female human beings. The question then arises: Why is maleness significant among the conditions which qualify a person to 'represent' the Christ in the ministry of Word and Sacrament?

In the last resort what this question asks is very simple. *Is the relation of a female to Jesus as the Christ essentially different from the relation of a male to Jesus as the Christ?* This is the form – and, in principle, the only form – which the question of 'equality of the sexes' takes in the context of Christian existence (i.e. of existence 'in Christ'); and it is the same, in the last resort, as the question, already discussed, of the denotation of 'us' in the expression 'God-with-us'.

Now where this question – as distinct from the formally

christological question – is concerned, the tradition has a great deal to say of a fairly direct sort, if not by way of extended theological reflection, then at any rate by way of practice. Most important in this connection is the simple and obvious fact that females are baptized; and that this sacramental action establishes them in a certain relation to God in Christ. What is this relation, then, and what are its implications for understanding the role of women in the Church?

The primary point which must be made here concerns the nature of the relationship to Christ which baptism seals. That relation is not merely one in which the faithful person receives from Christ a 'gift' which is distinct from and external to the giver. It may be said, and properly said, that baptism confers forgiveness of sins or the grace of justification. It is apparent, however, in the light of New Testament understandings of baptism, that such gifts belong to the baptized person in virtue of the fact that he or she is 'joined' to Christ, 'puts on' Christ, becomes a 'member' of Christ, is 'buried with' Christ, and so on. To be baptized is to be so associated with Christ in the power of the Spirit that one shares in his relationship to the Father. 'God sent the Spirit of his Son into our hearts crying, Abba, Father.'[21] Hence a later writer like Cyril of Jerusalem can with perfect justification observe that the meaning of baptism is simply sharing in the sonship of Christ, as well as in his death, his resurrection, and his power to conquer evil.[22]

It is obvious from these considerations that the custom of baptizing women has at least indirect implications for the problem under consideration here. That custom does not merely imply a belief that women may be 'saved', i.e. that their sins are forgiven or that they are proper recipients of sanctifying grace. It entails also the belief that women can and in fact do *share the identity of Jesus as the Christ*, that they are incorporated in him, the representative of the human race, and that in consequence Christ lives in them.[23] So it must be said that baptism establishes women, as it does men, in the role of *representatives* of Christ – persons in whom the reality of the Christ-life, of at-one-ment with God, is proleptically manifested.

As far as the meaning of baptism is concerned, then, *women have the same relation to God-in-Christ as men*. Moreover this relationship constitutes them not merely as beneficiaries of salvation, but as sharers in the identity of Christ – which means his sonship, and therefore his servanthood, his priesthood, and his prophetic and royal offices *vis à vis* the world. That they do not and cannot share the maleness of Jesus is, apparently, no obstacle to this relationship or to the ministry which it involves – and for good reason, as we have seen, since it is Christ's humanity, and not his maleness, in virtue of which he is God-with-us. Baptismal practice and christological doctrine here reinforce each other.

But what does all this have to do with ordination? For ordination is not baptism. It is 'another' sacrament altogether, and presumably therefore the fact that women are baptized says nothing in itself about whether or not they may be ordained.

It is true, of course, that ordination is 'another' sacrament, and that it establishes a person not as a forgiven and justified member of Christ, but as one who stands in a certain relation to the Church – a relation which constitutes the minister a *sacramental* person signifying the presence of the divine Word by which the Church lives. Nevertheless it must be asked what, apart from ordination itself, is required in order that a person may truly fulfil this sacramental role in relation to the Church. Furthermore, in asking this question one must keep in mind that while there are indeed more sacraments than one, they differ among themselves not in *what they ultimately signify*, but in *the manner in which* and *the purpose for which* they signify it. The grace and truth which are in the Word Incarnate are one.

One requisite for ordination is, and always has been, baptism. Moreover, the reason for this is fairly plain. It is not primarily a legal requirement of membership in the institutional Church. Rather it is a recognition that the primary precondition of the exercise of ordained ministry is not a natural endowment of any sort, but membership by grace in the New Creation which the Church itself signifies for the world. Only the person who is 'in Christ' can fulfil a sacramental ministerial role; for such a role strictly presupposes his or her involvement in that grace which is the gift of identity in Christ, himself the New Creature. This grace, then, is a necessary condition of ordination.

But is maleness also a necessary condition for ordination? It is at this point that the relevance of a discussion of baptism to the question of the ordination of women becomes apparent. The fact that women are baptized; that baptized women are 'in Christ' and share his identity; that in virtue of this identity they exercise a lay ministry which involves the 'imaging' and 'representation' of Christ in and for the world – these facts create a presumption that they are also capable of 'representing' Christ in the role of an ordained person. The presumption is further strengthened when it is recognized that the identity in which Christ is represented to world and Church as their salvation is not that of a male, but that of humanity as bearer of the divine Word. The New Creature is not, as we have frequently enough said, constituted by maleness; and there is therefore no reason to suppose that maleness is required for its 'imaging'.

Thus in the last resort the question boils down to this: *Is it the Christ of the baptismal mystery whom the ordained person represents, or a Christ who is in fact otherwise understood and qualified?* The Christ of the baptismal mystery – the Christ in whom the new order of creation is embodied and effected – is one in whom male and female, Jew and Greek, slave and free, share a single identity. Furthermore it is this Christ, and not another, whom the christological tradition clearly sets forth, by its insistence on the integral and inclusive humanity of the Word. To insist, then, that ecclesial priesthood must be male if it is to represent Christ, is to argue that ecclesial priesthood represents a different Christ from the one which the other sacraments of the Church embody and proclaim.

On these grounds, it must be concluded not merely that the objection to the ordination of women considered here fails as an argument, but that the premises which apparently ground it imply a false and dangerous understanding of the mystery of redemption – one which, if carried to its logical conclusion, would effectively deny the reality of Christ as the one in whom all things are 'summed up'.[24] Once this is recognized, moreover, it is possible to see that the ordination of women would constitute a ministry more fully expressive of the Christ it represents than the exclusively male ministry which has hitherto been maintained by the Church.

Notes

1. 'Represent', for example, may obviously mean things as widely different as 'witnesses to', 'acts as agent for', or even 'symbolizes'. Similarly, a person may be thought of as an *eikon* of Christ either morally, naturally, or functionally; and these different modes of imaging do not necessarily imply or include one another. Thus this *genre* of language as generally employed conceals some ambiguities of thought.

2. See, for example, S. Kierkegaard, *Concluding Unscientific Postscript*, trans. D. Swenson (Princeton, NJ, Princeton University Press, 1968), pp. 86ff.; and Kierkegaard, *Philosophical Fragments*, trans. D. Swenson (Princeton NJ, Princeton University Press, 1936), pp. 44ff.

3. For some brief discussions of this general line of thought, see A. Richardson, *History Sacred and Profane* (Philadelphia, Westminster Press, 1964), pp. 125-7; R.R. Niebuhr, *Resurrection and Historical Reason* (New York, Scribner, 1957), pp. 23-8; R.R. Niebuhr, *Faith and History* (New York, Scribner, 1949), pp. 105ff. See also K. Barth, *Church Dogmatics* I.1 (T. & T. Clark, 1955), p. 189: '. . . the Word of God meets us in a form to be distinguished from its content . . . the form as such signifies a "riddle", a veiling of the Word of God.'

4. John 1.14.

5. Philippians 2.7.

6. Hebrews 2.9.

7. Ignatius, *Ephesians* 7.2; cf. *Trallians* 9.1-2.

8. Justin, *First Apology* 13.

9. ibid., 21.

10. Hebrews 2.17.

11. Irenaeus, *Adversus Haereses* III.18.7.

12. See, e.g., Athanasius, *Contra Arianos* III.30 (in J.P. Migne, *Patrologia Graeca* XXVI, 387C). Migne's collection is hereafter cited simply as MPG.

13. Gregory Nazianzen, *Epist.* CI *Ad Cledonium* (MPG XXXVII, 181C).

14. Athanasius, *De incarnatione* 54 (MPG XXV, 192B).

15. Ambrose, *De fide* III.62 (in J.P. Migne, *Patrologia Latina* XVI, 627C).

16. Gregory Nazianzen, *Oratio* XXIX.16 (MPG XXXVI, 93C-96B).

17. *idem*, *Oratio* XXVII.17 (MPG XXXVI, 48C).

18. Gregory Nyssen, *Ad Ablabium, quod non sint tres Dii* (MPG XLV, 121A). The translation cited here is that of C.C. Richardson in *The Christology of the Later Fathers* (Philadelphia, Westminster, 1954), p. 259.

19. On the subject of biblical imagery for God, see the useful article of P. Trible, 'Depatriarchalizing in Biblical Interpretation', in *The Journal of the American Academy of Religion* XLI (March 1973), pp. 30ff.

20. This stricture, it should be said, must apply as emphatically to attempts to speak of the Divine as 'androgynous' in its nature, as it does to characterizations of the divine nature as male or female.

21. Galatians 4.6.

22. Cyril of Jerusalem, *Catechetical Oration* III, *passim*.

23. Galatians 2.20.

24. Ephesians 1.10.

SIX

Jesus the Jew and Women

Jane Williams

It is now probably an accepted cliché that Jesus was 'good with women'. Quite a number of the incidents that the gospel writers choose to show Jesus in action, Jesus relating to people who are not part of his intimate circle, have women as their protagonists. Jesus took women seriously, ministered to their needs, challenged them to go beyond their ideas of themselves; he shows, in fact, just the same attitude to women as to men. Moreover, it has been pointed out that he never scores off women, never tells jokes about them, or stories whose point emerges only if the audience shares the belief that women are basically comic.

In this he was not, of course, unique; in any society – however outwardly patriarchal – good, close, understanding, respectful relations between the sexes will occur, sometimes. But if Jesus' behaviour is, in some sense, a pattern and inspiration for ours, it is instructive for us to see which of his attitudes he formed in real contradistinction from those of his own society, because those things, in particular, are likely to be things that he *chose*.

So what was the attitude of Jewish society to women at the time of Jesus, and how does it compare with Jesus' own attitude, insofar as we know it? Both sides of the equation are slightly hazy; we have very little written Jewish material contemporary with Jesus, or even with the gospel writers. The Mishnah, for example, was only formalized at the beginning of the third century AD. Much of what it contains is, of course, very old, but we do not have a comprehensive picture of the development of ideas and practices, so that we cannot look at a chart to see just what Jews believed on any given subject at any particular time. Equally, the gospel writers entirely fail to tell us all kinds of things that we would like to know about Jesus. They select stories for particular purposes and put them in contexts which might lead to conclusions not inherent in the events narrated. Look, for example, at the very different role that the cleansing of the Temple plays in John's Gospel and in the Synoptics, just because John has it as the beginning of Jesus' ministry and the synoptic writers as the end of the ministry and the beginning of the passion. Or again, the gospel writers tend to tell stories about Jesus in relation to *particular* people, instead of pieces of connected exposition: 'What Jesus thought about Judaism . . .', and so on. We all know the dangers inherent in generalizing from the particular: if Jesus told the rich young ruler to go and sell all that he had, does that apply to the rest of us or not? Yet, given this editorial bias and selection process that has gone on in the gospels, there is still a surprising amount of evidence left to show that women did play a significant part, both as members and as onlookers, in Jesus' ministry, as the Church recorded it. How much should this surprise us?

Judaism, as a religion, had a fairly low view of women. Rabbinic commentary, like that of the Christian Fathers, laid the blame for the fall largely on Eve, the representative of womankind: Adam was seen as a great and tragic figure, more sinned against than sinning. An adult male Jew said as part of his daily prayers, 'Blessed be God, King of the universe, for not making me a woman,' because women, like slaves and Gentiles, could never really be fully involved in the Jewish cult. It was in view of their general weakness, mental and physical, that Jewish women were excluded from all but the smallest of roles within the public cultus; for example, women did not get called to read the Torah in the public gatherings for worship, while their menstrual 'uncleanness' automatically debarred them from priestly functions, since, according to the Torah, a priest must be holy and clean to offer the sacrifices (cf. Leviticus 15, 21, 22). Similarly, the privilege of obeying the full measures of the Holy Law was largely lifted from women: they were expected to abide by the negative restrictions of the law, concerning not killing, stealing, and so on, but not in its positive injunctions. (This applied equally to Gentiles: the general moral force of the law was felt to be universally available to all right-minded human beings. It was the extra strictures laid upon the Jews alone that made them the particular people of God.) Since women were exempt from many of the more detailed regulations they were, in some important sense, outside the religious family of Judaism - any law that carried a particular time specification, such as the requirement to pray three times a day, was not binding on women. In that sense, Judaism, as a religion, was very much a male preserve.

On the other hand, Judaism as a society was not wholly contemptuous of women, although it was undoubtedly restrictive. A woman's public and her private position were rather different: she was not expected to go out more than necessary in public, and when she did her head was to be modestly covered; in practice, this custom must often have had no more than lip-service, for women were often needed to work in the fields or help their menfolk with the running of family businesses, and if they were too rich or aristocratic to need to work, they also tended to stand rather loose to customs of propriety.

In theory women did not own anything, not even themselves. They were the property first of their father and then of their husband. Everything a woman owned or earned belonged to her husband or to her sons after her husband's death, although the marriage contract, the *ketubah*, did state that at least minimal provision should be made for a widow. Thus the formal position for women was one of total financial dependence but, once again, this was not always the case in practice; widows, in particular, often managed to get a fair degree of financial independence, as did women of wealthy families who kept the management of their property in their own hands when they married.

Within the family the position of the wife and mother was one of considerable importance. Although the basic unit of Jewish society was called the 'father's house', the continuity of the Jewish race was through the mother - Jewishness was inherited *only* if the mother was a Jewess (cf. BT Yeb. 23a, Nashim I etc.). The small child was given its initial and formative grounding in Judaism by its mother, and the mother was responsible for seeing that the strict and complex dietary law binding upon all Jews was adhered to. Thus the inner social cohesion of Jewish society was acknowledged to be dependent upon its womenfolk; the stories extolling the virtuous (and usually self-denying) Jewish wife and mother are many and varied. See, for example, the ghastly story in 2 Maccabees 7 of the mother who watches her seven sons die for the faith, exhorting them the while 'with good courage because of her hope in the Lord' (verse 20).

To summarize quickly, and no doubt over-simply, Jewish women played their main religious and social roles within the context of their families. In that setting, they could gain great respect and even power. Outside the family, in public life, they were not supposed to have any formal role at all, whether religious, economic or social. In practice, the necessities of everyday life made these restrictions impractical for poor women, while very rich women ignored them altogether (look, for example, at the goings-on of the women in the Herod family!). Moreover, even the expressly patriarchal Jewish writings and legal codes know of exceptional women whose conduct, while it would be improper under normal circumstances, is acknowledged to be the result of God's calling.

So the position of women in society at the time of Jesus was probably not quite as restricted as we might imagine from reading what Jewish legal and social codes see as the *ideal*, but, on the other hand, an up-and-coming young rabbi would probably be expected to be slightly more careful in his dealings with women than other men. Jesus was certainly watched in his handling of religiously touchy areas, and his dealings with women were certainly not 'by the book'.

Jesus in Public

As I mentioned above, theoretically, women were meant to go out in public as little as possible. Outside the home and the family circle, it was improper for a man to be alone with a woman (see, for example M. Kidd. IV.12), and particularly if the man were a scholar or a rabbi and actually entered into conversation with women in the streets (cf. b. Ber. 43b Bar.). Yet the gospels record a number of instances of Jesus conversing with women in a way that almost certainly occasioned a few raised eyebrows, and that always resulted in endorsing and affirming the woman concerned.

For instance, there is the story (in Mark 5.24–34 and parallels) of the woman with the flow of blood. This condition would have made her virtually outcast, as she would defile any one with whom she came into contact, even if they only touched something that she had handled. Every woman would have known what it was to be 'unclean' for one week in the month, but this woman, so Mark tells us, had had a constant flow of defiling blood for twelve years. This might help to explain the stealth with which she approaches Jesus; she was committing an act that might be considered selfish, defiling a rabbi while he was unaware of her presence. But, when challenged, she admits her fault, and the fear with which she did so tells us something of her own sense of her uncleanness, her expectation that her touch would be disgusting to Jesus. But instead of blame she gets praise, for her faith.

There is also the story of the woman with the ointment (Mark 14.3–9 and parallels). Here the physical contact between Jesus and the woman is more intimate, for she wipes his feet with her hair – which would never be uncovered at all, if her reputation were one of her prime concerns. Luke points up the story even more strongly by implying that the woman is a notorious sinner, known to Jesus' host (Luke 7.39). The emphasis then becomes rather different; just *because* she is such a great sinner, she has more need, and the more knowledge of her need, of Jesus' forgiveness. Mark, who has no special note of the woman's sinfulness, sees the act as one of prophecy and poignant love; this woman sees where Jesus is heading, and her early recognition of it makes her one of the witnesses to Jesus 'wherever the gospel is preached in the whole world'. Once again, a woman is publicly commended for her boldness in recognizing Jesus and acting upon her recognition.

Let us take just one more story in this category – that of the Syro-Phoenician woman (Mark 7.25–30, Matthew 15.21–8). Once again, this is not just a woman, which would be bad enough, but a woman of a particularly inferior kind, for she is a foreigner. The story shows Jesus apparently changing his mind because of the determination and wit of the woman with whom he is talking. She knows she has no rights over him, for she is a 'dog' not a 'child', but she is sure that Jesus has power and compassion enough for all, without stinting anyone. The gospel writers suggest that Jesus' mission went beyond the Jewish people in his own lifetime, and at the suggestion of a woman; this woman sets ajar a door that Paul was to knock down altogether.

These three stories are all about women who add to their femaleness other disabilities that make them among the most despised members of the human race, in Jewish eyes. It is the very desperation of their situation that takes them to Jesus, where they are praised. The gospel writers do not choose to show Jesus talking to respectable women very much. To represent Jesus' public relations with women they choose apparently the least presentable examples of their sex and show them being liberated by Jesus' power.

Jesus with Family and Friends

But if Jesus was singularly free and unembarrassed in his dealings with women who had no claim upon him other than that of need, what of those women whom he knew well and saw often, such as those on the fringes of his followers, or Martha and Mary, or his mother, who might be said to have the right to make demands upon him? What of the other womenfolk in his family and the families of his followers? It is extraordinary how uninterested the gospels are in the ordinary details of the lives of Jesus and his followers. Nothing that does not directly serve the narrative is included. We know Peter was married because he has a mother-in-law who is healed by Jesus. Indeed, it would have been unusual in the extreme for a Jew to remain unmarried, yet Jesus and all his followers might be leading lives of celibate dedication to the mission for all the gospels tell us to the contrary. This ruthless disregard on the part of the gospel writers of all that might be considered of 'human interest' is so marked that one can only assume that Jesus' mission was indeed one that forced people out of the ordinary patterns of life, in obedience to a stringent call. Perhaps the disciples went home from time to time, but their reception must have been frosty - they were certainly not putting their families first.

One can see something of this in the hints that the gospels give us of Jesus' relations with his own family. All the evangelists agree that Jesus' dealings with his family during his ministry were cool. Even Luke, whose lovely opening chapters are the basis for all our myths about the Virgin Mary, has Jesus saying, 'My mother and my brothers are those who hear the word of God and do it' (Luke 8.19-21 and parallels). Throughout his ministry, Jesus puts the claims of his message of the Kingdom of God above the claims of the family. He calls his disciples away from their homes, he warns that his message will divide people from those closest to them (Mark 13.12 and parallels); no other ties must be put first.

Only once do the gospels record that Jesus obeyed Mary in her role as his mother - at the wedding in Cana of Galilee; and even here he questions her judgement (that strange little question, 'Woman, what have you to do with me?' in John 2.4, really cannot be made wholly complimentary to Mary, however tortuous the exegesis). In Luke 11.27-8 Jesus rejects the implied praise of his mother's nurture of him: 'Blessed is the womb that bore you,' cries a woman, complimenting both Jesus and the mother who made him what he was. But Jesus gives no credit to Mary's mothering role - the only thing that can prove his worth is people's response to God through him; Mary plays no part in it, receives no credit for her son, unless she, like others, 'hears the word of God and keeps it'.

It seems that Jesus' message was felt to be one that laid absolute claims upon its hearers. No one is any longer commended for virtuous and unbending fulfilment of the requirements of the Jewish law but only for turning towards God and his Kingdom in the person of Jesus. Thus no woman has her religious role safely completed by being a good wife and mother; *first* she must be a disciple. And the evidence of the passion narrative and of Acts is that Mary discovered this and became a follower of her son, relinquishing her right to be honoured and obeyed by him, preferring to honour and obey God through him. It is in this context that the Magnificat most fittingly comes from Mary's mouth, for she put away her security in favour of God's will not just when she bore an illegitimate child but also when she gave up that child to God's will. The one religious role that Judaism recognized for women - in the home - is rejected by Jesus; he challenges his mother to become a disciple primarily, putting her motherhood aside.

This picture of Jesus forcing Mary to step outside the time-honoured role of rabbi's mother into one more directly related to her own resources and consent is reinforced when we come to look at Jesus' relations with his women friends, as the gospels portray them. It is John's gospel (11.1-44) that tells us in so many words that the family at Bethany were something special to Jesus, though Luke's narrative, in using the names, may imply that these were people who would be known to the earliest Church. Mary, Martha and Lazarus are unusual in the gospel narratives because they are intimates of Jesus, who yet were not part of his nomadic band of followers. Most of the stories we have show Jesus meeting strangers, changing their lives, and then either leaving them or calling them to follow him. Not so the family at Bethany, for Jesus comes to *them*, not they to him.

Luke's story is one of the famous stories about Jesus and women (Luke 10.38-42). Here again, the obvious role for a Jewish woman, the one Martha plays, of the good hostess, is put aside by Jesus in favour of a more committed one. We are told that it would have been very unusual for a Jewish woman to sit at the feet of a rabbi, like a student, receiving instruction. But Jesus not only consents to such a situation but commends it. Mary has taken an initiative; she has become a disciple in her own right, not just the woman who feeds the rabbi.

John's Martha and Mary story is rather different, For those whose hearts go out to Martha as she slaves over her hot stove, it is good to turn to John and see that for these two women, in their faith, Jesus brings life from the dead. But in this story it is Martha who is given the extra insight into Jesus' mission, for John makes her the recipient of one of Jesus' huge, unashamed claims: 'I am the resurrection and the life' (11.25). These two women make good symbols of Christian discipleship, because they were willing to believe - Mary in choosing for herself a new role, Martha in hearing and receiving Jesus' message of new life.

But we have very little more to go on. What became of Martha and Mary and Lazarus after Jesus' death and resurrection - a resurrection that they, above all others, might have expected? What became of the mother of Jesus in the early Church, after her one brief mention at the beginning of Acts? One thing seems clear: she did not become the 'mother of the Church', and that may have been part of the lesson she learnt from Jesus - motherhood is not the same as discipleship. What of all the shadowy women on the periphery of the gospel narratives? What did they hear and understand? Why was it some of their number, rather than the disciples, who stood at the foot of the cross, and returned afterwards to find the empty tomb? Without romanticizing or trying to turn hints into evidence, all that can be said is that women heard the call of Jesus as something requiring response from them too. It was not enough to service the mission - provision it with food and affection and homes for the men to come back to, as Jewish women had always done - they, too had to take up their crosses and *follow*. The very roles that Jewish society approved for them, Jesus challenged. Wives and mothers they may have been, daughters and sisters too, but just like the Twelve, or any of the men whom Jesus met on his way, they were forced either to put God first or to retreat from God's call, knowing the responsibility to be their own.

Christianity - a Religion of Slaves and Women

All the stories of women in the gospels, then, show that Jesus took women with complete seriousness, and that they entered into faith in him on exactly the same basis as the men who followed Jesus; the only thing necessary was commitment. Unlike Judaism, Jesus's message knows of no easy way in which the 'weaker sex' can become part-sharers; faith in him requires the same degree of exertion on the part of men and women. Nor were women brought into the Church by their menfolk; the gospel writers show that very often they got there first, showing more comprehension, often, even than the disciples themselves. Over and over again, the great truths about Jesus are revealed to and accepted by women, and the most obvious models of the perfect disciple are not the Twelve but the women at the cross. We have already noted that Martha is the one who hears and receives the knowledge of Jesus's life-giving power. And she draws from this revelation the right conclusion: 'I believe that you are the Christ, the Son of God, he who is coming into the world' (John 11.27). Among the Twelve only Peter makes such a confession, and immediately goes on to misinterpret it (cf. Mark 8.27–33). Again, in John 4, Jesus declares outright to the Samaritan woman at the well that he is the Christ. Just try to feel the impact of that story – here is Jesus alone with a woman (not done), a foreign woman at that (not even a Jew?), and he chooses to indulge in theological conversation (but women can't learn theology, can they?). John says, rather mildly in the circumstances, that the disciples 'marvelled', and well they might.

But the steadfast discipleship of the women around Jesus really comes to the fore in the passion and resurrection narratives. All the gospels agree that it was the women who stayed with Jesus at the cross, and the women who were the first witnesses to the resurrection. There has been considerable debate about whether or not women could, legally, be witnesses at all. On the whole, it seems they probably could; one woman's unsupported witness would not stand as evidence, but neither would one man's (cf. M. Sot. 9.8, M. Ket. 2.9). But that is not really the point. Of course the witness of the women was not credible to the world at large, but who would believe anyone, of either sex, claiming that a dead man had risen? The important thing about the witness of the women to the resurrection of Jesus was that it happened that *they*, and not the Twelve, were the ones who went to the tomb. For whatever reason, their faith in Jesus had not been shattered by the crucifixion in the way that the others' had. However fearful and grief-stricken they were, their love for Jesus did not disappear with the failure of the expectations they had had of him. Perhaps they had never expected him to be the Messiah of power, overthrowing the Romans; perhaps the very fact that Jesus had taken so much trouble with *them*, the powerless and unimportant, made them doubt that he really planned to set up his own empire in Israel. If the sin of Jesus' male followers was that they expected the wrong things, that, despite all they had seen of Jesus, they still expected wars, revolution and triumph, the sin of the women was that they expected nothing. They went to the tomb only to show the dead body the last respects they could, perhaps to take it away and bury it more fittingly. If the cross was a challenge to the Twelve's understanding of God's power, so was the resurrection a challenge to the women's understanding of hope. From that defeat on the cross God brought life, from the confinement of the grave he brought freedom; what constrictions in ordinary life, even the life of women, could then withstand such transforming power?

It is not without significance that Christianity was at first - and still is, in countries where it has not become identified with the civil powers - a religion that appealed to the poor and the less powerful. Very few of Jesus' followers, from what we know of them in the gospels, were wealthy or influential; they were not the religious leaders of their day. Jesus' message was an uncomfortable one, not calculated to attract those who had the world well-organized for their use already. Nor was it presented by a person with the right credentials. The Jewish society that makes up the background against which the gospels paint their picture is a society with a bewildered expression on its face as it looks on. Sometimes the bewilderment is good-natured; if only Jesus would give them a sign, they would give him their serious consideration, but they needed something to get hold of. Sometimes, as in the trial story, the bewilderment becomes savage and fearful, because to believe Jesus would be to break up a system that *worked*, a system by which you knew what God wanted of you and you could measure whether or not you had fulfilled your part; usually you probably had not quite made it, for Judaism has always known that God is very great and very mysterious, but at least you knew that you were on the right road: you knew what God was *like*.

The God Jesus presents is utterly unsystematic; even his notions of right and wrong seem a bit shaky. He demands response, commitment, love, and never lets you feel you have done enough. Such a God might well seem less threatening to those who had never felt that they had got it even nearly right before, anyway, those for whom the system did *not* work - the poor, the sick, and women. These people had less to lose, and Jesus' unexpected God sounded as though he sometimes let people in just because he liked them!

Jesus' death and resurrection took the understanding of the surprising God to even greater depths, for it destroyed human ideas of vindication and power and creativity. Jesus' death and resurrection are the events by which he is openly declared by God to *be* God, to be the place from which new life comes, and so they are the events by which God hangs a question mark over all other sources of 'power' and transformation, even over our own old ideas of God.

At its most basic, it is obvious that those without power are often the first to wish to see power structures fall, but also the first to assume the same kinds of power after the revolution. This is not what the resurrection is doing; it is not saying to the Jewish authorities and the Roman army, 'You had the right idea of power but looked for it in the wrong place, so now you will pay the same kind of consequences as you exacted from others.' The resurrection does not wipe out the cross by turning the tables on the executioners; on the contrary, by making the crucified one the central figure it suggests that questions about power are the wrong questions, that God's new life cannot be legislated for, that those who are least interested in justifying themselves *may* be the ones whom God will justify.

That is why the debate about the ministry of women cannot really be carried out along the lines of a debit and credit column: 'Jesus was certainly a man, but, on the other hand, he thought women were important; Jesus did not choose women to be part of the Twelve, but, on the other hand, he *did* choose them to be the first witnesses of the resurrection,' and so on. It is not even any good to be able to demonstrate that Jesus was unusually good to women by the standards of his day; the gospel writers note this, certainly, and the earliest Church almost certainly practised a good deal more equality of the sexes in religious matters than might have been usual in Judaism - they even had women ministers, according to the Pauline epistles, though quite what is meant by that we cannot know. But Jesus irritatingly failed to legislate about these matters, and the

97

Church had to make up its own mind about how they thought he would have run things if they could have consulted him face to face. The growth of church organization has been, on the whole, a very hit and miss affair, partly guidance, partly practicality, partly inherited ways of doing things. To search the New Testament for phrases that might suggest that Jesus would have established an episcopacy is to misuse the record we have of the way God worked in Jesus and the way in which people responded to him. Similarly, to count verses for and against women taking authority in church is asking God to *legislate*, to give us an easy set of rules by which we may know his mind. But all that the gospels give us is a picture of a life, death and resurrection and the impact that it had on those who witnessed it. It is a picture that notably dwells on the poor and the sick and the outcast, to the point where Jesus' death actually makes him one of them. It is a picture that is shockingly hard on the rich and the powerful and those satisfied with their religious observance, however well-meaning and sincere they might be in this. It is a picture that differentiates and evaluates people *only* by their response to the central character. Jesus' message, is, according to the gospels, an intolerably uncodifiable one. All that can be said is that any laws that protect your own interests at the cost of your love for your neighbour must go; anything that you value above God keeps you from him utterly; the only form of kingship is through service: look for the ones who serve most and there you will see the kind of leadership that God recognizes. The cross shows us that human power and fear warp humanity and make it small, but also that they cost God dear. Human power put God on the cross, human fear that God should not be the kind of God we want, God the King. The resurrection shows us that God is free of our ideas of him and that we too can be free of those fears that nailed him to the cross, that we can be free of the need for power over one another and God, and can grow up 'to the measure of the stature of the fulness of Christ' (Ephesians 4.13), until race, sex, respectability, are no longer the test, but only willingness to serve God.

Over against the Jewish society of his time (and against our own society, come to that), Jesus chose, the gospels suggest, to assess people by quite new means. All kinds of marginalized people found themselves closer to God than they could have suspected under the old rules. The gospels hold these people up, the lepers, the mad, the tax-gatherers and sinners, the dubious women, as symbolic for us of the ways of God, partly *just because* they did not imagine that God was made in *their* image. God is always unexpected, always pushing the boundaries of our imagination of him further and further. In choosing his company and the recipients of his power from among the lowest of his society, Jesus showed something of the lawless grace of God, his endlessly humbling love that will not be satisfied, even should the Church show its own love to and through women priests. Always God-in-Christ seems to demand, 'Do you love this person, or this group or this thing as I do? Will you risk yourself for it, as I do for you?' And if the answer is shown to be 'No': be prepared to be changed.

Useful Reading on Jewish Society

Encyclopedia Judaica, see under 'Women', etc.

J. Garcia and S. Maitland (eds.), *Walking on the Water* (Virago, 1983, essay by Maureen Gilbert.

J. Jeremias, *Jerusalem at the Time of Jesus*, SCM, 1969.

R. Ruether (ed.), *Religion and Sexism* (Simon and Schuster, 1974), particularly the essays by Phyllis Bird and Judith Hauptman.

E. Schüssler Fiorenza, *In Memory of Her*, SCM, 1983.

B. Witherington, *Women in the Ministry of Jesus*, Cambridge University Press, 1984.

SEVEN

Crumbs from the Table: Towards a Whole Priesthood

Anne Hoad

'Yet even the dogs under the table eat the children's crumbs.' (*Mark 7.28*)

Several streams of thought circle around our present notions of priesthood. There is a whole debate about its nature and purpose. There is the question raised by the lives and experience of women about the validity of confining priesthood to the male sex. There is the search for a renewed priesthood. It is not within the scope of this article to deal with such a rich and varied debate. However, from the whole range of material I want to pick up one area of concern which is crucial for women.

Many of us who minister within the Church find that our experience of God brings us into conflict with aspects of the Church's traditional teaching about priesthood. I believe the most satisfactory way to proceed from this impasse is to look afresh from a feminist perspective at the New Testament, to see whether an interpretation can be found which will speak to women's experience at the present time.

Although we cannot return to Christian origins, we do need to hold a conversation with the past to see whether dialogue can assist the development of a woman's view of priesthood and whether it is possible to find a way of discovering evidence of women's power and real involvement in the events of Jesus' ministry. We can and do need to grapple with the theological significance of the role of women as portrayed by the early communities, and to consider what bearing this has on our understanding of priesthood for today. Then we need to test out what promise our viewpoint holds for women, who like men are created in the image of God, and who are seeking space within the Church where that promise can be fully lived as a reality. Lastly it is important to determine the nature of the change required of us if we are to shape our vision of a whole priesthood into a continuing community inclusive of women in the future Church.

My aim then in thinking about priesthood and about the hope of its redirection and renewal is to start from the dissatisfaction and unease that has emerged from women's groups inside and on the edge of the Church and from that perspective to see what questions are thrown up for our consideration. Feminist theologians start from women's experience as a major platform for inquiry. The cornerstone of their theology is a belief in the validity of women's experience today, not as a matter of prevailing fashion, but rather as one way in which God is revealed in the world, and chooses to engage in the human situation. The development of women's consciousness has highlighted the all-pervasive maleness of priesthood and we have reached a crisis point in the history of our Church when to a significant number the developed tradition as it relates to priesthood seems inadequate and inflexible. The restatement of the old tradition is of little avail. So are the attempts to return to the older traditions of the Fathers.

To begin with it is essential to sketch out from whence the conflicts with the Church's traditional teaching and practice arise, to try to uncover the source of women's struggle to evince a changed response from the Church. There are many analyses which taken together make up a feminist model describing male society and women's place within it. Patriarchal religion is widely regarded as reinforcing women's powerlessness by ignoring their experience in the past and present, by speaking of God in the male image and by promoting systems of dominance that damage women. I have chosen an analysis which starts by examining carefully the social arrangements between women and men, which proceeds to study the psychological consequences flowing from them and which identifies the positive qualities which are thereby available to all from women's situation. Jean Baker Miller in her book entitled *Toward a New*

101

Psychology of Women[1] demonstrates the fixed nature of these structural relationships as well as the way women are encouraged to develop the characteristics which keep them fixed.

Her study opens up the first of two main areas of conflict which I want to focus on - women's second-class citizenship in the Church.

There is nothing new in defining women's situation in a male-dominated Church as oppressed. We have been tradition-ally designated the humbler members of Christ's body, able to represent Christ in the world by virtue of our baptism, but unfit to represent Christ as priests. There are many relationships of temporary inequality, in which persons are socially defined as unequal - parents and children, teachers and students, vicars and curates, therapists and clients. The aim of these relation-ships is to bring an end to inequality by the passing on of desirable qualities to enable a person to grow to maturity, but as women we are placed in a permanently unequal relationship. In this relationship, like that of class or race or nationality, we are defined by birth. The superiors in such relationships do not see themselves as needing to raise up the inferiors. Indeed the normal goal of seeking to move through to a more equal state is usually denied. The dominant group guards very carefully the functions it enjoys performing and labels the subordinate group inferior, 'naturally' suited to less desirable tasks which, in women's case, extend far beyond what is biologically determined. Subordinates are said to be unable to perform the preferred functions by reason of apparent innate defects of mind or body and therefore no change is possible. They are encouraged to develop characteristics which oil the wheels of the existing arrangement - submissiveness, dependency, in-ability to act, decide, think. These characteristics are more like those of children - nevertheless the subordinate is considered adjusted if he or she acquires them. In fact, if such people develop functions like intelligence or initiative there is no room for the acknowledgement or use of them. Furthermore, culture or society's overall outlook legitimizes in its morality, theology and social theory this unequal relation. It is normal to demean others because the effect of what is happening is hidden and is not recognized or examined. To keep the relationship in being you only have to continue doing what appears normal. All the open power and authority is held by the dominant group who determine the way power may be acceptably used, though this is masked by the development of the belief that they know what is best for others and that really both sets of people have the same interests at heart at all times. Direct action to redress the situation can result in economic hardship, social ostracism and psychological isolation.

If we set Jean Baker Miller's analysis against the present relationship between groups of women and men in the Church far too many of her observations strike chords in our experience. Many women live happily with the Church's present arrangements and accept the theological concepts of women's place which underline them. However, an increasing number find this acceptance more and more impossible, especially as a genuine women's theology and critique emerges. The theology which has been developed as a defence against arguments in favour of the ordination of women attaches immense significance to Jesus' maleness and profoundly affects our understanding of the universality of redemption, and wider theological issues. The relationship of Christ's maleness to priesthood becomes an untouchable mystery on a metaphysical and symbolic plane. The underside of such theology, and of theology developed from patriarchal texts within the New Testament, is that women continue to be seen as only representing the creaturely side of humanity with a minor role in the outworking of redemption, whilst the doctrines of submission and subordination are reworked with new vigour. It therefore becomes ever more difficult to recover a ministerial view of priesthood which embodies the whole Church. And more difficult, too, to discover a view which will enhance women's freedom and power, not for the purpose of controlling others, but for the sake of effecting a wider, more human vision and application of the gospel.

The women who question the subordinate role assigned to them and still remain in the Church seek a new concept of womanhood and adulthood which will free them from permanent tutelage. Nothing is new about applying the message of

103

the gospel to struggles for greater freedom. This has been done before in relation to circumcision and slavery. What appears to be so disturbing to many people is when the liberating message of the gospel is appropriated by women in their situation today. 'For freedom Christ has set us free; stand fast therefore, and do not submit again to a yoke of slavery' (Galatians 5.1).

In practical terms the strictures of the old unbalanced relationship of women's life in the Church are painful to us, and it has been the courage of those women who have refused to remain quiescent that has opened our eyes to our situation. There is a long inventory of problems to be faced: the control of theology and theological education in the Church has been in male hands; selection for ministry is on a male model; resources and administration are largely directed by priests and some selected laymen. Women's participation in responsible posts and even in the General Synod is minimal. A recent survey on the position of experienced women parish workers and deaconesses for the Church Pastoral Aid Society[2] showed that a proportion of those in authority would not consider giving women a post which involved sole charge. Many jobs are linked to sacramental responsibilities which means that women cannot find responsible roles, and even where posts could be made available they are not in fact being released. Jobs are tied to male appointments so that most work for a woman is insecure. The survey showed that one in five women questioned had seriously considered leaving the ministry.

The second main area of conflict surrounds lost history. The actions of women in past times are rarely preserved by the prevailing male culture and little preserved in the Church. So quickly do the gains which are made disappear from sight that it becomes difficult for women to locate a supporting tradition and history. Constantly, new starting points have to be found despite the fact that the raising of women's consciousness has a much longer history than people generally realize. What we need to search for is the distinctive experience of women, so that we can develop a tool for historical analysis. We need to look at women as the initiators and makers of history not simply at how they complement a history already evaluated and written. Whilst women bring their own values and judgement to their experience in the Church these remain unexplored, because they do not have any influence on the direction of Church policy or any access to favoured publicity outlets. From a woman's standpoint events will be evaluated in a different way from that which has been accepted by a male culture. It may prove, for instance, that when women's history in the Church is written the growth of women's theology and vocation in the present will be more accurately seen as a reformation for us than the male-designated reformation of the sixteenth century.

The reclaiming of our distinctive history is deeply symbolized by the role of woman priest as celebrant, and that is why so much difficulty surrounds the Eucharist itself. As a priest she is recalling, in the same way as men have done, that inclusive history and sacrifice of Jesus which invites all humanity to struggle with and be sustained by God: as a woman she is saying that the body of Christ, the community of the Church, welcomes the memory, aspirations, and history of women in which Christ has and continues to become incarnate. Thus we women can proclaim that we are fit to reflect the image of God, and to offer our bodies as a living sacrifice. The remembrance of the inclusive history of Jesus is so central an act that any theology which seeks to alter it, or any issue, be it maleness, femaleness, blackness or whiteness, which loses sight of it will become either permanently or temporarily unconnected with the potential for wholeness.

But the scandal or stumbling block that needs to be deeply opposed is that the very community solemnly charged with spreading before us this saving history of Jesus obscures and hides in practice the loving invitation to everyone which lies at its heart. It is not surprising that it is a theologian from the Third World who has most accurately described what this deprivation means, 'Even if the majority of women are not conscious of these issues, the more alert and dynamic among the women dedicated to the cause of Christ feel that there is here a discrimination of a sexist nature. They are thus hurt in their deepest being. They are torn between a respect for the

Church and their inability to accept such treatment from a community which should foster equality and solidarity.'[3]

For these reasons the idea of priesthood holding out any hope or promise for woman is totally rejected by many. The negative theological definitions, and the organizations which maintain them, are largely in the hands of priests and women's questioning puts them at odds with the power of the institution. To seek spirit-filled communities, marginal to the church, and a prophetic, critical role for women and women's theology seems the only positive option open. It is rightly pointed out that the promises of God are directed towards a future kingdom rather than an institutional Church. This response has very important consequences for the Church. At the centre of the controversy lies the authority and meaning of priesthood.

When we try to move towards a conversation with the biblical material, with the aim of shaping a woman's view of priesthood, huge difficulties emerge. Our concept of priesthood today has arisen from an historical process evolving within greatly varying cultures, many of which held a very limited, and sometimes hostile, view of women. Its authority is derived from length of practice rather than from forms irrevocably laid down from the beginning. It is also noteworthy that there have been real discontinuities in its development. When we examine the practice of Christian priesthood as it has developed in the Church of the present day, and turn to the pages of the New Testament for confirmation of the present interpretation, we can be in no doubt that a great deal has changed. In a society full of the symbols of the old priesthood – a caste priesthood, perpetually offering sacrifice for people who could not do it for themselves – there comes a new starting point – Jesus. He was not a priest in the meaning of that term in his own day, and yet his life and ministry are the source for a new and evolving tradition of how Christian priesthood is exercised.

The new starting point offered by Jesus brings about a whole new effort of interpretation and starts a new conceptual struggle. Looking back to the New Testament, we get fragmentary glances of how the writers were coping with this tension between the old and the new. The complexity and variety of the biblical contexts makes it impossible to be precise about how far the old is preserved or the new added, but if we look at how the Old and New Testament writers used past traditions and how they fashioned new and lasting ones a pattern emerges which is important for the current debate. Their relationship to the past is dialectical but, as the old traditions are given new content and meaning which goes beyond previous interpretation, then feelings of radical discontinuity arise. Commitment to a struggle between the old and new in which the reality of the old is held in dialogue with the lived experience of its reshaping becomes very difficult. In practice such a dialogue cannot be truly achieved unless both parties to it, who hold known theologically valid positions, are allowed to live out their positions in mutual respect within the community of the Church.

If we are to explore what is the nature of Jesus' new priesthood then we must turn to Hebrews. It is a very mysterious book, difficult to understand. The testimony of Jesus' life and work – as pioneer suffering leadership – the offering of a whole life (Hebrews 2.10) leads the author (or authors) to draw some conclusions about Jesus' place in relation to the tradition. The emphasis is on what is new and discontinuous. All the evidence of experience suggests that Jesus is the unique priest of a new covenant, who offers life for all. Yet he is not part of the professional class of Levites. The author wrestles hard with this problem in chapter 7, verses 12-16:

> For when there is a change in the priesthood, there is necessarily a change in the law as well. For the one of whom these things are spoken belonged to another tribe, from which no one has ever served at the altar. For it is evident that our Lord was descended from Judah, and in connection with that tribe Moses said nothing about priests. This becomes even more evident when another priest arises in the likeness of Melchizedek, who has become a priest, not according to a legal requirement concerning bodily descent, but by the power of an indestructible life.

The new starting point, which Jesus offered in terms of priesthood, raised the problem of the tribal barrier concerned as it was with designation by birth. The author argues that the barrier was overturned in order to introduce 'a better hope' (Hebrews 7.19). To justify this radical discontinuity the author turns to the obscure proof text about Melchizedek, who is interpreted as representing a new kind of priesthood, independent of the old Levitical tradition based on lineage, thus no longer equating priesthood with the old sacrificial cultic figures, but with a new royal priesthood (taken up in 1 Peter) inclusive of the people of God. Jesus, then, is the model for new and evolving traditions of priesthood. His priesthood was a radical break with the past, which we can say came in a way and from a quarter not experienced before, so that we can be encouraged to look for new forms of priesthood away from the places where it might be expected, not simply to an archetypal past.

We are not therefore alone in struggling with the difficulty of looking to the past when our relationship to it may only be partial. However huge the task, we should not be put off in an attempt to reclaim the history of women and to take a fresh look at the evidence of women's power, activity and real involvement in the events concerning Jesus and to grapple with the theological significance of the role of women as portrayed by the early communities. In turning to the gospels I am aware that my milieu is the kitchen and playroom, not the study. Using the biblical material the social and historical background of the early communities, and the place of women within them, is extremely difficult to unearth. The records are, of course, exclusively male, often speaking of women in passing. Yet the task of reconstructing the historical experience of women has to be done from them. In addition there is the painstaking task of weighing the relative importance of the various strands of text and the struggle to understand the social context. Nevertheless, I am cheered by the recognition that in the gospels we are reading early attempts to share a vision, as well as attempts to interpret the significance of Jesus, which are deeply coloured by the experience and commitment of the people who write.

So I need to try, despite the difficulties, to discern from the memories and reflections of the first communities and individuals the signs of women's inclusion and participation in discipleship.

Because of the limited space available it is only possible to draw out the threads of women's participation in a broad sense. Nevertheless, it is clear that women were active in perceiving the newness of Jesus and his proclamation of a kingdom for the outcast. The good news was tremendously attractive to them with its emphasis on the poor, the sick and crippled, the sinners, tax-collectors and prostitutes. Since there already were a group of people, the guardians of the Temple and Torah, who thought they knew exactly how people should think of and approach God, those who were excluded from the circle of the elect and holy had most to gain from Jesus' message. And women were amongst those most oppressed by the proscriptions of the Holiness Code.

Women's perception and recognition of a new kind of authority in Jesus was by no means passive. His challenge to an apparently settled and rigid way of thinking resulted in a hot debate about God, and it is not surprising that, given the priorities of Jesus' ministry, most direct confrontations in the gospels were with the religious authorities of his day. So women's ability to recognize newness and power in Jesus is very important. The woman with a haemorrhage (Matthew 9.20-2, Mark 5.25-34) recognized, despite her fear and guilt from years of feeling unclean, that she would be made well if only she could touch him. Jesus laid hands on a crippled woman – she stood up straight and praised God (Luke 13.10-17). In John's gospel Jesus' discussion with the Samaritan woman leads her to ask people to test whether this could be the coming Messiah (John 4.7-30). Martha proclaims Jesus as 'the Christ, the Son of God' (John 11.27). Mary of Bethany (John 12.1-8) anoints Jesus with costly perfume as the last act of Jesus' ministry in anticipation of his hour of death and glorification. These are women who identify and perceive God's new presence and immediately recognize the significance of what is happening before them. Luke describes women taking the initiative in ministering to Jesus; they accompanied him as he went round preaching in the villages and contributed their resources to the mission (Luke 8.1–37). They also use their authority to make claims upon him. This is highlighted in the story of the Syro-Phoenician woman. Her young daughter was polluted by virtue of an 'unclean spirit', and because she was a Gentile (Mark 7.25–30, Matthew 15.22–8). She asks Jesus to heal her child. His response that the children of Israel must be fed first is countered by the woman's own claim for a portion of the meal.

Above all, the gospel writers show that women found the resource to stay with Jesus at critical moments of conflict. They stood by him at his death. That they chose to do so was not an act of pious devotion, but a decision that in the circumstances would have been considered very carefully indeed. Elisabeth Schüssler Fiorenza points this out in her book *In Memory of Her*.

> Mark uses three verbs to characterize the discipleship of women under the cross: they *followed* him in Galilee, they *ministered* to him, and they *'came up with him* to Jerusalem' (Mark 15.41). The women are thus characterized as true disciples of Jesus who have left everything and have followed him on the way, even to its bitter end on the cross.[4]

We have, in addition, the strong traditions of women present at the empty tomb, still deeply involved in the last events. Later, in the gospel tradition, they were given authority as the first witnesses of the resurrection to proclaim the message of the risen Lord first revealed to women disciples in a vision. In John's Gospel, Mary Magdalene is portrayed as the primary apostolic witness to the resurrection – she went to the disciples and said, 'I have seen the Lord' (John 20.18). Here is an example for all followers of Christ of one who seeks and finds the Lord.

Thus women were witnesses and disciples. It is also noticeable that men and women carry different strands of tradition. The significance of this is unclear. What we do see represented is the authority of women in selected gospel stories and traditions. This, then, is the direction in which we must explore – these are the tools. As yet our glimpses are partial and much work needs to be done before the implications can be fully worked out.

When we turn to the writings of Paul we have very little direct reflection or information on Jesus' life to go on, but in broad terms the same features of ministry appear in his record of the early Christian communities. He appears to regard himself as the focus of a group of co-workers commissioned to share in the work of mission (2 Corinthians 1.21; 8.18-19,24). We also have a picture of how he saw the wider purpose of ministry. His reflections on the meaning of Jesus' death and resurrection lead him to state that all ministry is founded on the redeeming act of God in Christ (2 Corinthians 5.18-20). Therefore he commends his own work and that of his co-workers, 'fellow workers for God' (1 Corinthians 3.9), on the basis that it enables the Church to carry out its work to the world (2 Corinthians 5.12-15; 4.13-15). (See A.T. Hanson's book, *The Pioneer Ministry*.[5])

Women were amongst these fellow-workers, or were established in ministry before him (Romans 16.1-16; Philippians 4.2-3), and were warmly commended by him. They contributed to public worship. Elisabeth Schüssler Fiorenza[6] argues that women could emerge as initiators and leaders of the missionary movement where it had started before Paul's conversion. Nevertheless, there is no certain way of discovering what Paul's own attitude to them was, because of the inconsistencies of the record and Paul's apparent ambivalence about their proper conduct. It is also not clear how far the Church's adaptation to the patriarchal patterns of the Graeco-Roman world had advanced.

The evidence of the early communities and individuals brings up the inescapable question for women, as to whether the way in which this pattern has been expressed and the way in which the text has been wielded, has hidden the earlier message by its patriarchal forms. To quote Elisabeth Schüssler Fiorenza:

In historical retrospective the New Testament's sociological and theological stress on submission and patriarchal superordination has won out over its sociological and theological stress on altruistic love and ministerial service. Yet this 'success' cannot be justified theologically, since it cannot claim the authority of Jesus for its own praxis.[7]

When we look at what bearing these questions have on our understanding of priesthood and its practice, we would expect certain features of Jesus' ministry to reproduce themselves and to be central to its authority: the giving of life to God; the knowledge of what service is; the ability to suffer and bear the cost of conflict; the showing forth of the signs of the risen life so that its power can operate to release the oppressed and welcome them to the free following of God. Jesus called people to follow him so that they in their turn could carry on the redeeming action which he initiated. But those who were closest to Jesus at first were not so much required to be like him in any particular natural way as required to do what he did (Mark 3.13-15; 6.7-13) and to be with him in sharpest conflict (Luke 9.28; 22.8; Mark 13.13; 14.33). By the operation of these criteria women in the past, and many we know today by the testimony of their lives, have that priestly authority, though unrecognized by the Church.

If it is true from the biblical pattern that we would expect the priesthood to live out the suffering and vulnerable life of Jesus, it follows that we would also expect the absence of elements of the old type of priesthood which are based on power for certain groups. Priesthood, as we learn from Hebrews, comes from God through the spirit for the benefit of the whole Church. It is not *possessed* by any group of people, nor any individual, nor even by the Church by itself.

In practice we have a system of priesthood which sharply divides the vocation of clergy and laity, and which is largely focused around the cult. The new starting point Jesus offered, as portrayed in Hebrews, centres around the unique, and once and for all, nature of his sacrifice. As the people of God our whole vocation, both laity and clergy, is to manifest priestliness by living in a sacrificial way, rather than by cultivating a tribal and cultic priesthood implying that certain things can only be done by one class of people. Our joint task is to give living reality to, and to evoke, the priestliness of humanity. The laity are uniquely placed to display and discern those qualities of altruism which are evident as people give life sacrificially for each other in birth and death - the task of interpretation is to make the links between that process and the sacrifice of Jesus which is embodied in the Eucharist.

As women in the gospel and women today clearly show forth the gift of sacrificial living and altruistic service, it follows that their participation in the mission of Jesus is significant for the reshaping of our notions of priesthood. It is important to notice that it is not simply the male text that is a problem, but also male interpretation. Only now, as we look from different angles, can the significance of women and their part in ensuring the presentation of the risen Christ to the world through the Spirit, be brought to bear on the question of the joint direction of the Church and its leadership. So future forms of priesthood will spring from the development of women's theology. If we are to join together to recover a concept of the priesthood of the whole Church with participation at every level according to the distribution of gifts (Ephesians 4.4-16), with ministerial priesthood expressing the body of Christ both female and male, then women's ordination cannot be denied.

With these background thoughts, the pressing question for women is whether there is any hope that the Church's priesthood can be regarded as genuinely inclusive of them.

On the one hand, there may be some hope in the future that the recovery of a concept of ministerial priesthood, in which the priesthood of the Church is invested and represented by the official priesthood, holds out the possibility of an inclusiveness being given to the term 'priest' which would be accepting of and acceptable to women. On the other hand, many Christian feminists are very sceptical of the value of women gaining admission to the priesthood. Perhaps this scepticism is best summed up by Rosemary Radford Ruether: 'Women win inclusion in this same ministry without asking whether ministry itself needs to be re-defined.'[8] The difficulty of this debate is enormous, since it springs from the deep alienation women feel within the Church once they have started to apply the liberating message to their own situation.

113

It is precisely when feminists discover the congruence between the gospel and liberation from sexism that they also experience their greatest alienation from existing churches. The discovery of alternative possibilities for identity and the increasing conviction that an alternative is a more authentic understanding of the gospel make all the more painful and insulting the reality of most historical churches. These churches continue to ratify by their language, institutional structures and social commitments the opposite message.[9]

This conflict becomes heightened at the Eucharist where Rosemary Radford Ruether speaks of 'starvation of nourishment'.

Many women draw the conclusion that an alternative, counter-cultural role and ministry for women is more express-ive of the faith. However, in the long term, an alternative ministry and a prophetic role which is not in real dialogue with tradition cannot provide the necessary shelter for the handing on of the history of women and, as Rosemary Radford Ruether herself points out, is not ultimately stable enough. We need to work with others to form the communities which will cherish and pass on the struggle for women's life, freedom and growth. We need to live out the basic gospel which is graciously addressed to all human beings in its fullness and signifies, in terms to suit the future, that female and male persons are included in that loving communication. Ultimately, the rep-resentation of both sexes in priesthood adds to the universality of Christ's promise and redemption: making it, piece by piece, more recognizable and perceptible to all.

Another similar doubt often voiced is that women's partici-pation in the present structure 'under male rules' brings no real change. Women, Ruether stresses, 'are allowed success only by being better than men at the games of masculinity, while at the same time they are rebuked for having lost their femininity. In such a system it is not possible for women to be equal, but only to survive at tremendous physical and psychological cost'.[10] But in the long run, to view the Christian feminist community in a way which separates it from strivings for renewal within and on the edge of the Church diminishes it. One of the basic beliefs of women's theology is the interconnectedness of all oppression, whatever historical problems there are in making those connections. There is also a price to be paid, of a different kind, in belonging to the priesthood or the Church as a black person or if you have working-class origins. Fundamentally, we are faced with the task of identifying wherein lies the embracing love and inclusiveness of the promise of God for ourselves. But this cannot be done honestly if we and the Church have not first faced the negative reality of our oppression. Our reflection upon God's promise is absolutely central because therein lies the hope, far off maybe, unseen maybe, of our new meeting – the hope of a true relationship between women and men, of mutual relatedness and interconnectedness. And where the community is so fractured, so defended that the task becomes impossible; when for some the inclusiveness of that love becomes hidden from sight and the tasting and the seeing is no longer nourishing, then the memory of Jesus, deeply careful to remove the burdens from 'the little ones', who are so weighed down by the requirements of religious duty and law, is still our inspiration and a promise to be realized, although at present we fail.

Women have much 'hidden treasure' resulting from their situation in the Church and the world. The very qualities which have been produced by the arrangements which keep women in second-class citizenship can yield the potential for the positive development of a theology of mutuality and interdependence. Ideologies of mastery and control no longer suffice for our world. The recognition that our resources are limited and are desperately needed to sustain all the peoples of the world means that we have at some point to learn new ways of using and sharing them; co-operation is more important than competition. The potential for destruction through nuclear holocaust reminds us of the cost of nurturing life and bids us take on board responsibility for the fate of the earth.

The purpose of women's theology is not to supply a women's page for the *Church Times* or to deal with women's problems as a marginal addition to what is going on very nicely already. By contrast, its aim is stated by Elisabeth Schüssler Fiorenza:

. . . traditional academic scholarship has identified humanness

115

with maleness and understood women only as a peripheral category in the 'human' interpretation of reality; the new field of women's studies not only attempts to make 'women's' agency a key interpretative category, but also seeks to transform andro-centric scholarship and knowledge into truly human scholarship and knowledge, that is inclusive of *all* people, men and women, upper and lower classes, aristocracy and 'common people', different cultures and races, the powerful and the weak.[11]

The depth of the change required of us and the scope of the task is daunting - so much so as to seem limitless. What attitudes can we adopt?

Where can we start? Strangely from the situation which brings us so much pain. I believe we can try to live freely and lovingly within the situation of powerlessness even as we struggle to change it and as we participate in the struggle with God. If we can live fruitfully within the narrow confines of our present situation, then we are free to respond to the power of God and free to address ourselves to one basic question - is God creating a new event in our midst?

Even as we seek to reflect on the question, there are some pitfalls to avoid. It is all too easy to adapt to things as they are and to avoid real involvement by seeking those therapies which take personal healing as their only priority and thus bring about withdrawal from public and corporate struggle. Although we know that the virtue of humility is essential in our approach to God, we must not acquiesce when it is recommended as a total life position for one class of people ensuring their perpetual subservience and thus spiritualizing the *status quo*.

It is also important for us as women honestly to face the pain of our situation in private and public. 'If we cannot name our experience of pain and anger,' writes Nicola Slee, 'we cannot release the sources of energy and vision within us. Part of our struggle as Christian feminists is to find a way of naming this pain and desire which is at once constructive and prophetic, healing and releasing for the *whole* Christian Community.'[12] If we can give voice to our pain we shall find life and power. Power not for the purpose of oppressing others, but to effect a new vision. We will discover the resources to do this because of our

116

powerlessness, because we belong, however small our problems in comparison to some of our sisters, to a servant community which has met every need that male society has devised, has washed its feet and cleaned up its mess. As individuals within such a community our weakness can be transformed into strength.

'Who has believed what we have heard? And to whom has the arm of the Lord been revealed?' (Isaiah 53.1).

We do not know if this is God's moment - we can only travel blind, preparing the ground as if it were - if it is not, our work will be inherited by others. The recognition that we are a sacrificial and servant community will lift up our heads and, at the right moment, if we prepare the ground, the full affirmation of the redemptive and priestly role of the servant community of women will come about so that we can make the distinctive contribution to the whole priesthood we long for.

The Syro-Phoenician woman (Mark 7.28) freely claims a full part for those outside the table fellowship of Israel. Her challenge to Jesus wins wholeness for her daughter, and her intelligent and truthful argument meets no defensiveness in him - only praise for her faith (Matthew 15.28). A Gentile woman with access only to crumbs from the table inspires the vision of a new wholeness.

Notes

1. Jean Baker Miller, *Toward a New Psychology of Women*, Penguin, 1976.
2. Survey on the Position of Experienced Parish Workers and Deaconesses by Dss Judith Rose.
3. Tissa Balasuriya, *The Eucharist and Human Liberation* (SCM, 1983), p. 53.
4. Elisabeth Schüssler Fiorenza, *In Memory of Her: A Feminist Theological Reconstruction of Christian Origins* (SCM, 1983), p. 320.
5. A.T. Hanson, *The Pioneer Ministry*, SPCK, 1975.
6. Fiorenza, op. cit., pp. 101 and 161.

7. ibid., p. xx (Introduction).
8. Rosemary Radford Ruether, *Sexism and God Talk: Towards a Feminist Theology* (SCM, 1983), p. 200.
9. ibid., p. 193.
10. ibid., p. 201.
11. Fiorenza, op. cit., p. xx.
12. Nicola Slee, 'Parables and Women's Experience' (*Modern Churchman*, New Series, XXVI, 2, 1984), p. 31.

EIGHT

Mary: My Sister

Jill Robson

I am a Roman Catholic, but not from the cradle. I was born and baptized in the Church of England, took in Protestant principles with my mother's milk, and was weaned on the Book of Common Prayer. Later, many things attracted me to Roman Catholicism, mostly its universality, its continuous history, and more than anything else, the mystical tradition that spoke to me of a reality that I knew for the first time – a pearl of great price for which it seemed to be worth selling all that I had. As far as I was concerned, Mary, and devotion to her, was *not* part of what attracted me, irresistibly drew me, to the Catholic Church. In fact the complex ramifications that has been built up around Mary, the mother of Jesus, left me feeling a strange mixture of bewilderment, incredulity and mild revulsion. I did not understand how such a complicated edifice could have grown out of the simple biblical stories which I had grown up with and which I thought I knew and understood. Nevertheless, Mary, her Immaculate Conception and her Assumption, along with papal infallibility, appeared to be an essential part of the package. I was quite sure that for me God was speaking most clearly through, and drawing me into, the Catholic Church. So I took a deep breath, a large gulp of (holy?) water, and swallowed the pill, hoping that in time I would come to appreciate the fullness of Mary. For I could see that many holy and wise women and men, whom I admired within the Catholic Church, had a great and living devotion to her which fed them spiritually and gave them important insights that I lacked.

In the meantime, I accepted that I was a Catholic with good Protestant gut-reactions, even though I had formally abandoned some of the principles which had formed those gut-reactions. I decided that as I could not accept Mary as 'Mother', nor as 'Our Lady', then all I could do about her was to accept her as a mother-in-law figure, that is, as the mother of someone very important to me, whom I loved dearly, and to whom I was committed for life. This was by no means a negative attitude, as I had at that time just acquired a real mother-in-law, a woman who loved and accepted me as a daughter from our first meeting, but who did not interfere in the relationship that was developing between her son and I. She seemed to me at first a woman whom I could love and respect, but who was important to me because of her relationship to the man I loved. As a person, as a woman, her life and ways seemed far distant from mine. They were good and loving, but were not of the shape I intended and expected my own life to have.

Over twenty years I have grown in depth of love with my mother-in-law, and have come to see her life as a woman, although set in a different time and subject to different social pressures, as having more to say to me that I had ever imagined it could do. In many ways it is contact with feminism and the women's movement that has opened my eyes and ears to the powerful truths that my mother-in-law's life so loudly proclaims.

Strangely, almost the same things could be said of my relationship with Mary. There has been a growing in awareness of how her story has been used as part of a particular set of ideas and concepts about women that have been implicit, both in the Church and in society in general.[1] And also there has been a growth in the understanding of how the biblical basis of her story has been used in a particular way, which has had much more to do with the current social attitudes to women than with anything else.[2] Slowly I have come to see how my gut-reactions were in fact better informed than I realized at the time. Now, it is by understanding what it was about the way Mary was being used (and which I was reacting to, rather as I was reacting to the surface features of my mother-in-law's life), that I have been able to appreciate that behind the stereotypes and pious plaster saint there is a real woman whose life can speak clearly to me, and from whom there are deep insights to be gained about what it is to be a woman responding to God in the ordinary circumstances of her own life.

I have moved from finding Mary presented in a number of ways I found emotionally and temperamentally difficult to take, to an unexpected acceptance of her as Mary, my sister. That is: a woman with her own story, in whose experience I can find real points of contact with my own. Mary has for me become a 'sister' in the strong feminist sense of the word, with its overtones of solidarity and support. It is the story of how this change in my perception of Mary has come about that I want to retell and explore.

I want to explore my own reactions to Mary for several reasons. First, I think that my instinctive reactions are shared by many English people, and are formed by a mixture of Protestant attitudes, the insights of the Reformation, along with our phlegmatic and non-emotional national character. So I hope that what I have to say of my own experience will accord with that of other English people. Secondly, I hope that by taking examples of mariology which I personally encountered, and by exploring how I reacted to them, I can now, with rather more informed hindsight, demonstrate some rather larger themes. My third reason for talking about my own experience is that of deep-rooted feminist conviction that 'the personal is political': it is where our own lives are touched by larger outside movements and forces that politics really begins. But in this case, 'the personal is theological'. My last reason for discussing my own experience rather than more generalized ideas or abstract notions, is a passionate belief that Christianity is about incarnation, where God touches our bodily lives, where he speaks to us through our bodily, daily, ordinary (and extraordinary) *experiences*. And this is often most *clearly* articulated by story telling, as the Bible very obviously shows.

Hail Mary: My Introduction to Her

Due to quirks of the educational system, my parents' social mores, and certain rather dramatic changes of staff in the private girls' school I had been attending for four years, I found myself, aged about fourteen, catapulted into a convent school. I was the only new girl in the Upper Fourth, which was bad enough, but to suddenly find myself surrounded by *Roman Catholics*, and being taught by *nuns*, was really very frightening. (This was in the days before the calling of the Second Vatican

Council, and we were all very unecumenical and ill-informed about each other in those days.) I had all sorts of unformed and nameless fears and prejudices about Roman Catholicism, picked up, no doubt, from the ways that my parents spoke about the church-going of our Catholic neighbours. I had also picked up the idea that Catholics engaged in all sorts of strange practices, the nature of which had never quite been explained to me, but which were only darkly hinted at during history lessons and confirmation classes as being what Luther and the Reformers were protesting about.

After the initial shock of being dropped into this alien convent environment, my first reactions were of amazement: 'My goodness, they are Christians too!' (As I said, we were very unecumenical in those days!) Nevertheless, there certainly were things about the practice of Catholicism in this new school that I did find very different from the practice of Anglican Christianity that I had grown up with. These differences were very largely in relation to Mary. Suddenly Mary, the mother of Jesus, Mary whom I had known of chiefly through the Christmas story and the birth narratives in the gospels, this Mary had become Our Lady, Our Mother (no, not *my* mother!). Suddenly this biblical character had become a very important focus of attention and devotion. To me this was to blow her up out of all proportion to anything I had ever thought about her.

Previous to this, the only ways I *had* ever thought of Mary, other than at Christmas, was as the mother of the boy Jesus, perhaps bringing him a drink and a biscuit in the workshop at Nazareth, or as the rather over-anxious mother who had lost him in Jerusalem: both rather Sunday-school attitudes. Mary was a biblical version of Alice who looked after Christopher Robin and took him to see the changing of the Guard. I can see that such an attitude to Mary was much conditioned by my middle-class background and was interpreting her in line with the current social expectations of women. She seemed to me to be the same sort of kind, loving, available, resourceful mother who figured in the 'Listen with Mother' stories, or who hovered in the background of the children's books I read, a mother who was there to help the main characters get on with their adventures. (I think I had probably seen the life of Jesus as some sort of rather good adventure story.)

Now, given that sort of unconscious mind-set, those sorts of implicit ideas about who Mary was, you can well imagine my shock at finding I was expected to *pray* to Mary *three* times a day at school. That amount of public prayer was bad enough, but to pray to *Mary* was almost an offence! There was the Angelus, the Rosary, the prayers to Mary at assembly every morning, the hymns to Mary, and statues of her in almost every classroom (all of which had a crucifix) and in the corridors and other odd corners. It was all too much! It felt very foreign, very strange, and my Reformed principles arose within me and asked, 'Isn't this idolatry?'

I think I would have answered 'Yes' to that question if I had judged by the practice alone, but there was also the theology, the teaching about Mary. Mary was the pattern for *all* believers, because she heard and responded to the word of God. It was obvious to me that there is something very important here. Mary did play a uniquely important part in the history of salvation. She was prepared to take an enormous step of faith and say a complete 'Yes', a complete '*Fiat*', as she stepped over the edge of the abyss. I could see that she took a huge risk, which is scarcely possible to quantify in retrospect, when she said:

> Behold, I am the handmaid of the Lord; let it be to me according to your word.

I could see that such an action, born out of complete faith in God, does deserve to be remembered.

So my reaction to the first half of the 'Hail Mary' was that it was all right.

> Hail Mary, full of grace, the Lord is with thee.

So far so good, this is biblical and what the angel said. Then:

> Blessed art thou among women, and blessed is the fruit of thy womb, Jesus.

Well, that's OK too, and it's roughly what Elizabeth said, but it's funny putting the emphasis on Mary's womb, rather than on Jesus. But

> Holy Mary, Mother of God, pray for us sinners, now, and at the hour of our death.

That is all much more difficult.

I could see that there is something important here that I had not previously been aware of. Mary, a woman, an ordinary if rather special human being, carried God in her own body, and it was out of that human body of hers that God took flesh. I could see that there is a real insight here: that God takes flesh, becomes a man, through the co-operation of one woman, who, through her body, gives him humanity and brings him to birth. I came to see that this was very much worth celebrating, and that the title 'Mother of God' was appropriate, even if it sounds very alien and strange on Anglican ears. I later learned that the early Christian form of this title was *Theotokos*, which can also be rendered 'God-bearer'. Perhaps this Greek word captures more of the incarnational and co-operative nature of Mary's part in the enterprise than does the bald English rendering 'Mother of God'. After all, if God created all things then he can't have a mother!

I came to see that the attitude of the Roman Catholic Church to Mary had real insights to share with me which my Reformed background had not exposed me to. *But . . .!* But, I still felt uneasy. I think that I jibbed at four aspects of Marian devotion: Mary as 'Our Mother', Mary's perpetual virginity, Mary as 'Our Lady', and Mary as part of the Holy Family.

Mary Our Mother

The reservations I had about 'Mary our Mother' are twofold: emotional and theological. I encountered this aspect of Mary when I was in the middle of my adolescence, when I was having quite enough trouble negotiating my relationship with my own real-life mother, trying to separate myself from her and to discover who I was. I certainly did not want to take on a larger-than-life heavenly mother (who presumably from her celestial vantage point would be able to know what I was up to *all* of the time!). So my first reaction to this aspect of Mary was emotional, and by extension I found titles given to Mary like 'Mother of Mercies', 'Mother of the Church', 'Mother of Priests' and 'Mother of Good Counsel' difficult to relate to, although I could see that perhaps some people found them comforting.

I found my emotional reaction was most strong to some of the hymns that we sang at school, for instance, this hymn, written by Saint Alphonsus (1696-1787):

> O Mother blest, whom God bestows
> On sinners and on just,
> What joy, what hope thou givest those
> Who in thy mercy trust.

> *Chorus:* Thou art clement, thou art chaste,
> Mary, thou art fair;
> Of all mothers sweetest, best;
> None with thee compare.

The verse I found the most unbearable was:

> O Mother, pitiful and mild,
> Cease not to pray for me;
> For I do love thee as a child
> And sigh for love of thee.

Well, that sentiment might be all right for an eighteenth-century, noble-born, ex-barrister, Neapolitan priest who founded a new order – he could afford the luxury of being Mary's child, it probably gave him the emotional security and child-like trust we all need. But for a teenager struggling to become her own woman it felt very oppressive.

My second reaction was a theological one. In the teaching I heard about Mary, there was always a very clear distinction made between the worship of God and the veneration of Mary and the saints. God alone could be worshipped, for he, as we know, is a jealous God. So prayer, adoration and worship are for God alone. If this is directed towards any other created object, however good in itself, then this is (at least the beginnings of) idolatry. Jesus, as God incarnate, can therefore be worshipped, but Mary, as a human being, can only be venerated with love and affection. I could see this distinction; it was clearly in line with what I knew of the ten commandments, and of the Old Testament interdicts against idolatry. *If* this was how Mary was being honoured, then that was, theoretically, acceptable.

But from what I *saw* of the devotion of others (and it was therefore just their behaviour and what they said, for I did not see what was present in their hearts), I could not distinguish between the worship of God and the veneration of Mary. In fact, to my phlegmatic English eyes and ears, the enthusiasm for Marian devotion seemed to me to be most unnatural. People seemed to pray to Mary with much greater ease and alacrity than they did to God. They seemed to expect of Mary all sorts of miraculous powers and the ability to grant prayers: attributes that I thought belonged only to God.

There were several phrases in hymns that I found particularly disturbing, for instance, this well-sung favourite of our school (a hymn written in the twelfth century by Bernard of Cluny):

> Daily, daily sing to Mary,
> Sing my soul, her praises due;
> All her feasts her actions worship,
> With a heart's devotion true.
> Lost in wondering contemplation
> Be her majesty confessed;
> Call her Mother, call her Virgin,
> Happy Mother, Virgin blest.

Or another oft-sung hymn (by John Wyse, 1825-98);

> I'll sing a hymn to Mary,
> The Mother of my God,
> The Virgin of all Virgins
> Of David's royal blood.
> O teach me, Holy Mary,
> A loving song to frame,
> When wicked men blaspheme thee,
> To love and bless thy name.

This last is plainly a piece of propaganda written in the nineteenth century when the Church felt the need to defend itself from the understandable criticisms of the Reformers. I refused to sing it – teenage priggery! Nevertheless, I can now see that there is something odd and worrying about the inconsistency of teaching a theology that says one thing and singing hymns that say another, although, of course, this is not a problem unique to the Catholic Church. Since that time, the effects of how ideas and attitudes, implicit within the language (for example, as used in public worship), can shape people's understanding, self-concepts and thought-worlds, have been clearly demonstrated.[3]

I think that lurking behind my teenage reactions was a genuine uncomfortableness that Mary was in some way being used as an object of worship in some sort of mother-god/mother-goddess way. Somehow I felt that God was coming off rather badly. In retrospect, I think that there may well be something in this.

Mary has to some extent been treated as if she is more than human, or at least, as if she was part of the élite company of heaven. (She has, after all, according to Catholic tradition, been bodily assumed into heaven, and crowned Queen of Heaven.) Somehow this human woman has become a 'divine' being, and so her human, womanly qualities have been lost in some sort of idealized mother-figure. By taking her up into heaven and crowning her there she has been removed from ordinary people, and especially from ordinary women.

I am now deeply sceptical about this process. It seems to me as if men are separating off the 'good' aspects of mothers, and are putting them at a safe and idealized distance, making Mother safe, in an attempt to produce a perfect female, loving and kind, constantly on hand, one who cares and prays for you continually, and who does not have all those troublesome features of either sexual arousal (about which more follows), or the dominance and power of real women and mothers. Mary becomes some Supermum in the Sky. (Every man's dream? Perhaps some women's too – we could all do with someone like that on occasions!)

The theological effect of this psychological process is that, in popular practice, Mary is made the advocate for sinners, and is made the intermediary through whom people pray, because she is human, but also in heaven. She will ask her son and he will grant requests. This seems to me to have moved Jesus into the Father's role as Judge – a role called into question by parts of the Johannine tradition (e.g. John 12.47) – and to have removed the emphasis on him as advocate with the Father (John 14.16 and 1 John 2.1), as our unique intercessory priest (Hebrews 7.25). And certainly this process has distanced the idea of Jesus as brother (Romans 8.29), and as a man, like us in all things but sin (Hebrews 4.15).

Not only has the position of Jesus been thus moved further off, but also, I think, this process has impoverished our ideas and ways of understanding God. The feminine, the good motherly bits of women, have been concentrated in Mary, who has been turned into some rather unreal, idealized woman who has then been promoted to heaven where she is seen as Queen, Mother and Bride, in contrast to God as King, Father, Judge, Bridegroom, Mighty Warrior, and so on. This has meant that there has been a polarization: the powerful 'male' roles are being used as images of God's nature, whereas the good female motherly, nurturing, caring, sustaining bits of our human experience have been concentrated in Mary. But although Mary is in heaven, she is not God.

I suspect that this is another (unconscious?) product of male psychology (the same process would apply to any dominant group), that is, they have projected onto God (or especially concentrated on seeing in God) those aspects of their own experience which give them power and status. They have been unable to see God as being manifest in ordinary woman, or to conceive of God as having those attributes of ordinary women that are scorned by society at large. Historical and social forces are such that we tend to see and think of God in images and metaphors that are current in our social thought and world. So although the Bible speaks of God making humankind male and female, and making them in his own image (Genesis 1.27 and Matthew 19.4), yet the patriarchal society of the Church has concentrated on the male aspects of God, and has ignored female aspects of God, or has just not entertained the idea that God could possibly have female aspects! So when they have come across female references to God, or female imagery, they have either ignored it[4] or said that it was a reference to Mary.[5] This process of repression, projection, displacement and stereotyping has had the effect of trapping women and of distancing them from an intellectual understanding of God. (Luckily God's nature is such that s/he is not limited by our understanding, and often rudely erupts into people's lives and experience!)

Mary, Ever Virgin

When, as a teenager, I first encountered the Catholic insistence on Mary's virginity, I found it almost incomprehensible; in particular, all the teaching surrounding her perpetual virginity, the belief that Mary conceived and gave birth yet remained a physical virgin, and that she remained so throughout her life, having no further children. It is only fair to add that the perpetual virginity of Mary is not a defined Catholic doctrine, but only a widely held pious opinion.

I remember us making our RE teacher, Sister Grace, go pink with embarrassment when we pressed her, by asking 'naive' questions, to explain (away?) the references to the brothers and sisters of Jesus in the gospels (Matthew 13.54-6; Mark 3.31 and 6.2-3; John 7.3,5).[6] I was frankly incredulous when I was told that Mary suffered no pain during childbirth. 'Well, wouldn't she be rather whacked after such an experience anyway?', I remember asking the rapidly reddening Sister Grace. I was prepared to believe that Mary had a particularly good experience of childbirth, but not that it was totally unlike what any other woman experiences.[7] That, it seems to me, diminishes the incarnation. So far, the inner meaning of the Immaculate Conception of Mary has not been vouchsafed to me; I still find the reasons for the promulgation of that dogma baffling.

But in all of the (massive) writings, speculating and theologizing about Mary's virginity, and the very central place it seems to have taken in both Marian doctrine and devotion, I am suspicious of just what is going on. It seems to me that Mary's ordinary female sexuality is being separated off from her motherhood - again, a way of making her into a safe, perfect, 'ideal' woman. So here is this woman who hears and responds to God's word to her (in a way that is centrally about her sexuality), by conceiving a baby in her womb. Yet the (male) tradition has taken hold of this story and embellished and interpreted it, to such an extent that it has created an impossible goal for women: a chaste, perfect, ideal, virginal mother-figure, a sanitized woman, a woman who is contrasted with Eve, who is then given the polar significance, the totally carnal (degenerate?), sexual temptress, through whom sin came into the world. (And that is not the emphasis given to the story in Genesis anyway!)[8]

Others have written about how women have suffered from this polarization of models of women into either Eve or Mary,[9] and I have very little to add to this here, except to emphasize that Mary is the logically impossible combination of virginity and motherhood. (I am not denying that virginity *can* have an important meaning, and can be a real, important and personally liberating way for a person, a woman or a man, to serve God.) But because Mary is a human being who completely responded to the will of God, she *ought*, I believe, to be accessible as a role-model for Christian women in general, whereas, in fact, by dwelling upon her life in the Communion of Saints rather than her life on earth, the Church has removed her from the realm of the possible. This has left women with the other pole, Eve, the type of the harlot, the temptress, or adventuress, who represents female sexuality, which is given a very bad press. This polarization has made women ashamed of their own sexuality, ashamed of their own bodies, which have become associated with sinfulness (unless bodiliness is denied or cut off by virginity or prudery). And I suggest that this has been put onto women by men. It is men who have gone on about it, who have written and pronounced upon Mary's virginity and Eve's guilt. Why?

Again, we seem to be observing a process of projection onto others of experiences that are difficult or painful. (Well, of course it's her fault that I am upset; I didn't do anything!) Men in patriarchal societies are in charge, are powerful and strong. In states of sexual attraction and arousal they are not in complete charge of their own bodies, or their emotions, and may well find themselves dependent on a woman's whims and emotions (which may well bring with it unpleasant memories of childhood dependency on a woman). Also, in states of sexual attraction, a man may well find his stronger exterior crumbling, and a much softer, weaker side of his nature may come out. Now, I realize that this is no news to anyone. But if that sort of expression is against all the norms of the society that you live in, then it has to be accounted for in some terms, and a convenient way is to blame the other person for the effect that they have on you. So in sexuality a woman's place is in the wrong. Just as slave owners or plantation owners often complained about the lack of moral fibre of their slaves or workers, which made them discontented or work badly, so we often think that the fault must lie, not with ourselves, nor with the system we are part of, but with the personal failings, or personality faults, or lack of hard work or moral control, of the other persons. This sort of self-deception is natural enough. We all do it. But where it has happened on a large scale and has prevented women from discovering their true nature before God, it is a serious matter.

Our Lady

When I went to my convent school, and bumped up against the concept of Mary as 'Our Lady', I experienced further difficulties. Our Lady, the chaste virgin, the lady of the troubadours, Mary seen in the light of the tradition of the romantic love which came out of twelfth-century France - this tradition produced Saint Bernard's devotional writings on Mary, the *Salve Regina*, the rosary of Saint Dominic, the idea of England being Mary's dowry, and the iconography of the coronation of the Virgin as Queen of Heaven. For me, all of this was very foreign, and found no resonances in me, so that I was left unmoved. I could not see Mary in any way as a wonderful, distant woman to look up to, or as a queen to inspire crusades, or personal battles. Neither did I ever feel myself to be 'a poor banished child of Eve' - life was too good and rich to be described as 'exile in a vale of tears'. Mary was not my life, my sweetness or my hope; her clemency, sweetness and loving did not move me. Nevertheless, in later life the music of the *Salve Regina* does move me deeply, it just speaks to me of longing for God, which is perhaps what all of the cult of Mary as Our Lady is really about. Personally, I feel as distant from Mary as Our Lady, Queen of Heaven, as I feel from Guinevere, Queen of Camelot, or the Lady of Shalott.

Mary and the Holy Family

The last aspect of Marian devotion I came up against was a different nuance in Mary 'Our Lady', where she was presented as a member of the Holy Family, that is, Mary, Joseph and Jesus, living at home, in peace and good order in Nazareth. When I went to my convent school (which was dedicated to the Holy Family), I discovered all sorts of stories about the family life in Nazareth. Interestingly, these were rather different in tone from those that I had heard at Sunday school. The effect of this contrast, and the lack of any biblical evidence for the stories, which became apparent to me at the same time, due to concurrent study of the gospel texts, was to make me discount both sets of stories as apocryphal tradition, myths, or the equivalent of fairy stories. But the interesting thing was that Mary, as portrayed as part of the Holy Family, had all the virtues of a middle-class, bourgeois, nineteenth-century housewife. Demure, modest, self-effacing, she looked after her man, was a good housekeeper, ministered to the poor and needy, comforted the dying, etc. This model of Mary was often used, probably unconsciously, as a means of shaping girls' behaviour into ways that would be socially acceptable in middle-class society. For instance, a girl caught whistling was told that in doing that she made Our Lady cry! The advice given to girls going out with boys – itself a risky and rather dubious business, but the world was changing – was to do nothing that would make Our Lady blush!

Not having been brought up as a Child of Mary, and not having had these sorts of stories told me since my infancy, they had very little effect on me. My socialization had already gone on in rather different ways. Also, in the early 1960s expectations and social mores were changing very fast. I was not really touched by these aspects of Mary as a model of what a young Catholic woman should be. And in fact, in discarding these obvious nonsenses I discarded a great deal else of Mary.

Mary, a Sister

For many years Mary remained for me a remote figure, distant from me except through her connection with the Son, Jesus. In that period I became a wife, a mother, and I grew as a woman, coming to know more of who I was in myself and before God. This process was aided by my contact with the women's movement and Christian feminism, which did more than anything else to give me back my own experience of my life and of God, validated as being real and true and speaking of truth, my truth, the only truth I really know.

Strangely, it was one of the bits of the cult of Mary that was most incomprehensible to me that gave her back to me as a real woman, as a sister. It was through attending Mass on the Feast of the Assumption. Now, of all the bits of mariology that turned me off, none was so powerful as the Assumption. There are several very Marian priests at our church, which is dedicated to Saint Mary, so we had the works! In the sermon, the priest made a very striking remark: 'Mary's body was assumed into heaven because it was through her body that she was faithful to God's plan.' He then looked at the nature of her life. This set me thinking that perhaps the Assumption pointed to something very positive, and strangely it had something to say to me as a feminist that was not a big turn-off.

I am, however, still inclined to feel that the doctrine that Mary's body was assumed into heaven (like Elijah's and Enoch's) is part of the Marian tradition that produces parallels in her story with events in the Old Testament. Also, I think that this doctrine is an expression of the general tendency to 'spiritualize' or otherwise disembody the physicality and bodiliness of Mary's experience, and so to separate it from the ordinary bodily experience of other women.

What I want to do now is briefly to outline a few thoughts about how the gospel texts about Mary can be read by twentieth-century women. I am not for a moment thinking that in doing this I am actually engaging with the historical Mary – the real woman who lived in first-century Galilee. She is lost forever, except to the extent that she can be met in the Communion of Saints. Nor am I doing a biblical-critical job; that is the task of the biblical scholar and makes very interesting reading.[10] What I am doing is responding to the text that is there, and I am responding to it in the light of my own lived experience as a woman, and extrapolating from the text what might have been this woman's experience. This is twentieth-century feminist mariology. But it is, I believe, in line with the ancient tradition of the spiritual interpretation of Scripture, in trying to reach, through prayer and loving attention to the text, into the mind and purposes of God, and into the inner human reality that lies behind that text. It is the nature of the reality of Mary, as a woman, and how she responded to God's invitation, God's word to her, that I want to explore.

I was first struck by how Mary can be seen as a sister by my attention being drawn to the gospel for the Assumption which is from Saint Luke (1.39–56). It is the story of Mary visiting Elizabeth, her being greeted by Elizabeth and the confirmation, by another woman, of the validity of her experience of what God was doing in her life. This confirmation Elizabeth could give because of discernment that she made through her own body and the action of the child within it. Elizabeth calls Mary 'Blessed among women'. Mary herself celebrates the mighty work God is doing through her by singing the Magnificat (which is no gentle, passive statement seeking not to upset the *status quo*). This is a story about sisterhood.

Elizabeth called Mary 'Blessed among women', and the Church has echoed this cry down the ages and has seen Mary as uniquely blessed because of her faithfulness to her call by God. It is for this reason that she has become the pattern for all Christians. Her faithfulness was lived out through her body which had played such an important (and indeed indispensable) part in the plan of salvation.

So what was the form taken by the blessedness of the life of Mary? What was *so* specially blessed about it? Here is a woman who has a baby that is not her husband's (doubtless there was a lot of talk at the time). She was forced to travel away from home when her time came, and had to use an animal's feeding trough for a cradle. Political events meant that for the first years after this birth they had to live in exile, leaving in a hurry, travelling with the small baby, as refugees. She and her husband lost this child for three days when he was twelve. He was a strange, deeply thoughtful child whom she did not understand ('"Did you not know I must be in my Father's house?"' - Luke 2.49). She watched him grow up and pursue his mission in life, which, again, she did not really understand, and when she tries to help him, she is rebuffed ('"O woman, what have you to do with me? My hour has not yet come"' - John 2.4). Later, as his mission develops and she goes to see him (perhaps to try to suggest a course less likely to end in predictable disaster?), she is told that being his mother is unimportant ('"Who are my mother and brothers?" and looking at those who sat about him, he said, "Here are my mother and my brothers! Whoever does the will of God is my brother, and sister, and mother."' - Mark 3.31-5). And on top of that she had to endure the hurt of having the angel's words of promise to her, about the meaning and purpose of the child she bore, and her place in it all, turned upside down and thrown back at her by that very son in his mission - her body, her part, her self, apparently diminished and rejected ('A woman in the crowd raised her voice and said to him, "Blessed is the womb that bore you, and the breast that you sucked!" But he said, "Blessed rather are those who hear the word and keep it"' - Luke 11.27-8).

There were other women who were close to her son and travelled around with him, but she is never mentioned as being among them. She had to endure the pain and the shame of her son being publicly executed as a criminal. Watching your son dying slowly in agony on a cross can be no fun, and his handing you on to his best friend must be a mixed experience. She is not mentioned among the women who laid him in his tomb in any of the gospels, despite the tradition of portraying her with the body of her son across her knees. Neither is she one of the named women who went to the tomb with spices. Nor is she mentioned as one of the women to whom the risen Jesus appeared, although he appeared to a number of women and to his disciples. Hearing about all those things, which involve you more closely, more bodily, than anyone else, from other people who were party to the events when you were not, is a pretty uncomfortable sort of bodily and emotional suffering. Grief, after all, is very much a bodily matter. It is hard to know that someone else is doing what you most want to do – seeing, touching, weeping over the body of your dead son, and then to have other people see him risen, but not you, and finally, to have him disappear into the clouds, and still not have seen him – all this must be *very* hard. And to have gone on believing in God's good purposes through all that as Mary must have done (since the last biblical reference is to her being present at Pentecost when the Holy Spirit descended) – all that is quite some suffering.

It is in this life-history and in her faith in God's purposes, although it would seem that she often did not understand them, that Mary's blessedness lies. And because of her bodily faithfulness the Church celebrates Mary's special status. It seems to me (although it is quite likely that all sorts of other things were also intended), that this is a magnificent celebration of the importance to God of women's suffering, of women's bodily importance, of women's sexuality and motherhood, of their vulnerability and of their tenacity and stickability throughout apparent disaster, rejection, suffering and death. What the Church is asserting is the unique importance of the place that this woman's faithfulness through her bodily and emotional sufferings and joys, played in the history of salvation.

What do we find if we clear away all the pious clutter that adheres to Mary? – if we stop seeing her as a mother-goddess or an archetype of the feminine (which is often the-feminine-as-perceived-by-men), or as some impossible model to make women feel guilty and keep them in their place, or anything else she is turned into? If this is done, then we discover there is a real and very human woman, who lived a very human life, a life full of joys, sorrows and sufferings that hundreds of thousands of other women have also had to endure. This woman's faithfulness was manifest through her body and through her emotional life (which is particularly celebrated by the devotion to the Seven Sorrows that pierced her heart). It was through just those aspects of her life that women are most often beaten over the head with, in a distorted form, by men, as being their weakness and their shame – that is, it was through her carnality (bodiliness) and her emotionality (sufferings) – that Mary was faithful and gained her special place. And she did this not by denying her body, nor by suppressing her emotions, but by being faithful to the mystery of God's purposes and by travelling the way she had to tread through her body and through her emotions. And the Church celebrates this and shows that what has so often been seen as women's shame is in fact her glory.

Now, here at last is a woman I can identify with, whom I can perceive as an important role-model. To faithfully live out God's purposes in my life is what I chiefly desire, and it becomes increasingly apparent to me that this means my life *as a woman*. And being a woman, being human, means struggling with my emotions, discovering, owning and rightly using my sexuality. It means living my own life out in all its bodiliness and knowing that bodiliness to be *the* centrally important *physical* fact of my life, and the vehicle through which I relate to others (whether that is by cuddling my children, cooking meals for friends or writing philosophy). And it is the bodiliness of Mary's story that gives me encouragement. Mary also knew fear, rejection and grief, and through all of these only too well-known experiences, she was faithful. All of this gives me hope, and the feeling of solidarity and support: the feeling of sisterhood. I can now approach Mary and greet her, not only as the mother of someone centrally important to me, but as my sister, who is a woman like me in all the ways that matter most.

Notes

1. See, for instance, Marina Warner, *Alone of All Her Sex*, Quartet Books, 1978.
2. Rosemary Ruether, *Mary: the Feminine Face of the Church*, SCM, 1979.
3. The general effects of how language shapes thought and action was outlined in the pioneer text by Benjamin Lee Whorf, *Language, Thought*

and Reality (Cambridge, Mass., MIT Press, 1965). The effects of 'dead' metaphors, and images implicit in the language, is interestingly discussed by George Lakoff and Mark Johnson, *Metaphors We Live By* (University of Chicago Press, 1980). How language affects women has been explored by Casey Miller and Kate Swift, *Words and Women* (Penguin, 1976), and the application of this to liturgy is outlined in the publication by One for Christian Renewal, *Bad Language in Church*, 1983.

4. See, for instance, Isaiah 42.14b; 49.15; 66.12b.

5. See Ruether, op. cit.

6. See also Acts 1.14; 1 Corinthians 9.5; Galatians 1.19.

7. This view is the result of a very literal interpretation of Genesis 3.16, and therefore Mary as the New Eve is considered to be free of the curse, '. . . in pain you shall bring forth children . . .'.

8. See Phyllis Trible, *God and the Rhetoric of Sexuality*, Philadelphia, Fortress Press, 1978.

9. For instance, Susan Ashbrook Harvey, 'Eve and Mary: Images of Woman', in *The Modern Churchman*, 1982.

10. Raymond E. Brown, Karl P. Donfried, Joseph A. Fitzmeyer and John Reumann, *Mary in the New Testament*, Geoffrey Chapman, 1978.

NINE

Stereotyping the Sexes in Society and in the Church*

Henriette Santer

There are, as we all know, many signs of renewal and change in the way women and men live and work together in society and within the churches. We all could tell our own story about what has happened to us, that is, our own life's journey over (let us say) the last twenty years. And I expect that most of us would be surprised to see, if we sat down and took stock of our attitudes and circumstances as men and women, how much has changed in our own life, in our own attitudes and expectations, in our situation, in the way we feel people react to us, and we react to them.

Thinking of my own situation from some twenty years ago as a 'wife' at Cuddesdon to what it was some fifteen years later as a wife in Westcott House, it is clear that much had changed. The situation in Cuddesdon amounted to some sort of schizophrenic, double existence, with on the one hand the life of a professional woman, and on the other that of a wife on the periphery of, and basically excluded from, a quasi-monastic male institution. I thought then that in a church which does this to its people there is a definite and urgent need for change.

And things *have* changed. It is important to realize this: we are all involved in a process of change, we are changing ourselves and our circumstances are changing. Nevertheless, is there a need for further change? Many of us believe that, while acknowledging changes that have taken place, there is a need to change further. We even know in which direction we wish this change to go.

I would like to contribute something from another and

---

* Talk given at the MOW Annual Conference, Birmingham, 17 September 1983.

different perspective, that is, from the discipline of psychology, and to look at what psychology has to say about men and women in society and the Church. I obviously have to limit this. The field of psychology is wide. You know that if you were to ask two psychologists to speak on the same subject, you might end up with two completely different stories, depending on what theories they have based themselves on, and what they have selected as important. A Freudian or Jungian psycho-analyst, for example, would take the intra-psychic point of view: what happens in our psyche. Their views might be fascinating, they might well strike a chord, but they would be difficult to prove or disprove. They are speculative in nature.

I, on the other hand, propose not to be speculative but to stay with facts and findings. I will therefore base myself on the research evidence in the area of gender and sex-role develop-ment, and will comment on the relevance of this for our topic.

Is it true that we are still trapped in old attitudes and expectations? Do we still operate with different norms for men and women? Do we still hold stereotyped views of the sexes? I believe we do. There is perhaps a tendency in intellectual circles at present to see such stereotyping as a bit outdated. I fear, however, that the dynamics still very much persist. It is perhaps less blatant now - not so much of the 'women cannot drive' type - but it certainly still deeply affects our own thinking. Let me give just two illustrations of this as I described them in an article in *Theology* (July 1982). Both examples concern married couples, with equally well-trained and able partners. In the first example the husband was the charge-nurse of one hospital ward, his wife the sister of another. There was no difference in status, they were both good at their work. Then the wife was promoted to nursing officer, the husband was not. It soon became clear that the rest of the staff was worried: would this promotion cause a marriage crisis? For how would he stand it, his wife the acknowledged and openly recognized superior?! It is clear that had the husband been promoted there would have been no worry. The other example is of two psychiatric social workers. This couple was childless, but decided to adopt children. They were given a brother and a sister to adopt, both at the same time. To make the adoption possible, they decided to cut down both their respective jobs to half-time. The reaction of their friends was again revealing of the way we accept established patterns: there were expressions of admiration and sympathy for the husband (what an amazing man!), while the wife was thought to be rather demanding, someone who wanted to have her cake and eat it; she was lucky to have such a marvellous husband. Think also of many other commonly held opinions which, on reflection, have no other validation than that of stereotype. For example, husbands should be taller than their wives; a man ten years older than his wife is normal but a woman ten years older than her husband is odd; or a man should earn more than his wife and he should be preferably more, or at least, *as* able and intelligent as his wife.

An illustration of this more subtle way of stereotyping comes from a study done by an American social psychologist, Dr Matina Horner.[1] She used a projection technique to find out mens' attitude and womens' attitude towards success. She asked a hundred men college students and a hundred women college students to write a story following on from this sentence: for the men, 'At the end of the first term, John finds himself at the top of the Medical School class'; for the women, 'At the end of the first term, Ann finds herself at the top of the Medical School class'. The stories of these students were then, in true projective fashion, analysed. It was postulated, and I think this is fair, that the plot of the story and the way it is written contains some of a person's expectations and attitudes towards high-flyers like Ann and John. And what did Dr Horner find?

Ninety per cent of the men wrote positive stories about examination success: they described good future careers; the stories showed that they were comfortable with the idea of achievement; some implied that it might score them points with women. Sixty-five per cent of the women however wrote stories which indicated that the idea of success was anywhere from uncomfortable to outright terrifying. In particular it appeared that they felt that doing well professionally might jeopardize their relations with men. Many stories contained an element of concern: Ann would be isolated; she was in a dilemma having to choose between a career or a boyfriend. Some stories included the advice that Ann should do less well and should put her energies into backing up a male student who then in turn would do well and whom in the end she could marry. Some stories, the minority, were more aggressive in tone: Ann should not be so ambitious, she seemed a typical egg-head with whom everybody would get annoyed.

This piece of research is I think ingenious in that it does not ask men and women directly to say what they think of the problems of high achievement in women. One would get well-argued rationalizations. No, it tries to get at people's basic feelings about this. And that is what makes it interesting. It reveals how much these feelings are influenced by what are considered the norms for men and women. Matina Horner herself goes further and puts her research into the context of motivational theory. She postulates a motive in women to avoid success, a generalized variable called 'fear of success'. This interpretation is a bit more controversial, and there is no need to go into this here. What her research definitely does, is to give empirical evidence that our feelings towards achievement are quite different when thinking of men and when thinking of women, and are very much coloured by expectations, based on stereotype sex-role opinions. One may ask: What about the men, if they were to write stories about Ann, and women about John? There is of course less projection in such stories, less identification with the hero. Such stories would reflect more considered points of view. The few studies done in this way however show the same tendency, that is, negative imagery from the men about a high-flyer like Ann and positive imagery from women about John.

Another very recent study[2] throws an interesting light on how early these sexual opinions are developed. A group of 7- and 8-year-old girls and boys were told a story by their teacher one day, and were then asked the next day and also seven days later to tell the story back as far as they could remember it. In this story the teacher used traditional masculine traits when describing the girl (clear-thinking, dominant, forceful, tough, strong) and traditional feminine characteristics when describing

142

the boy (dreamy, affectionate, sensitive, etc.). It appeared that after one day, and even more so after seven days, the children would reconstruct the story in the direction of existing sex-role opinions, i.e. they described the boy as strong, dominant, etc. and the girl as sensitive.

Yet another interesting insight into sex-role stereotyping comes from a study in the field of mental health.[3] A large number of clinicians, psychiatrists and clinical psychologists, were asked to describe, with the help of a list of attributes, the ideal mentally healthy and adjusted adult, and then also the mentally healthy and adjusted male and the mentally healthy and adjusted female. It appeared that all clinicians, men as well as women, described well adjusted men as quite different from well adjusted women, but that there was no difference between the well adjusted men and the well adjusted adult in their description. In other words, there are two norms, one for men and one for women, with the mens' norm more ideal, and more socially and personally desirable. That is, the ideal man coincides with the ideal human being, the ideal woman with a pale reflection of this. It is interesting to note here, and we know that this is generally true, that women participate as vigorously as men in the depreciation of women and the limitation of the female stereotype.

To summarize this, yes, we are still stuck and trapped in sexual stereotyping. It still colours our expectations, our feelings, our attitude and even our memory. Secondly, the norms for men are more socially and personally desirable than the norms for women.

The next question is, I think, *not* how can we move away from all this; we will first have to ask whether sex-role stereotyping is indeed wrong. Is it perhaps based on reality, i.e. that women are basically different from men? Furthermore, does sex stereotyping perhaps have a function: does it help people to live more contentedly, more happily; does it structure our society in a basically beneficial way? I will now address myself to these two questions: Is stereotyping justified because it is based on real differences? – and secondly – Is stereotyping advantageous to the individual or to the institutions s/he lives in?

First then, are men and women different, do they have different abilities, different temperaments, different personality characteristics? Many studies have been done on the recording and documentation of differences as well as on the explanation of these differences. It is a vast field. At the risk of being over-simplistic let me just make a few points.

When it comes to the documentation of the differences, there are only very few variables on which researchers agree. On the whole, I think it is accepted that as far as our abilities are concerned, women perform best on tests of verbal skills, while men do better on tests of visual spatial ability, while, as far as personality is concerned, it is on the whole agreed that men are more aggressive and women more caring, that men are more easily frustrated and women more able to tolerate stress.[4] That is more or less the sum total of undisputed fact!

Let me make four comments. *First*, all studies that report differences set out to find differences. They do not concern themselves with similarities. If differences are not found, findings are usually not thought to be worth publishing. There is an obvious researcher bias in most studies. As two psychologists recently put it: 'Questions concerning the origin and nature of sex differences cannot properly be answered by and in a society that is predicated on their existence. And in a society not premised on their existence, we feel it unlikely that these issues would be a major concern.'[5]

Secondly, when talking about differences, in ability for example, we talk about *average* differences. There is of course an enormous overlap. Many individual women will be higher on a certain variable than many men. Take an example from another context: although the average man is taller than the average woman, I find myself taller than a great many men.

Thirdly, as for the explanation of these differences, how are we to know that they are biologically determined? Can they be environmentally determined? I have argued elsewhere (*Theology*, 1982) that it is impossible to separate nature from nurture, to separate what is given from what is learned: there is in fact a very subtle interaction between biological and environmental influences. In one study, for example,[6] it appeared that if a woman thinks, when playing with a baby, that the child is a boy, she will play more vigorously with it than if she thinks it is a girl. Now this in itself must have its effect on the future behaviour of that girl or that boy. In other words, *who* and *what* we are, and *how we behave*, and therefore also our differences in behaviour, are a product of our continual interaction with our environment.

Fourthly, and most crucially of all: If we are to accept that there are some differences, and I for one am happy to accept this, at least with the just-mentioned qualifications, can we therefore assume that these differences account for all the differences in behaviour, attitude and circumstances between men and women in our society as we see them? It is, I think, abundantly clear that we cannot. In other words, I think that it is important not to fall into the trap, when discussing differences between men and women, of asserting that there are no differences. There is no need to do this. The logical thing to say is that there might be some differences, but that these are average differences, and not necessarily inherent, and furthermore that they could not possibly account for the differences which are actually found in society. One could go even further and say: Even if there are differences, does this in itself mean that men and women ought to behave on the basis of these differences? The answer is 'No': facts don't imply values; what *is*, is not the same as what *ought* to be.

This brings us to the second question asked earlier on: Do sexual stereotypes have an adaptive or a pathogenic effect on an individual's development, do they help or do they hinder? It seems to me from anecdotal evidence alone, from what I see in myself and in others, that sex-role stereotyping can hinder development both in men as well as in women. Think back, for example, to clever Ann and her perceived dilemma. Think of the anxieties, guilt or just the inhibitions a child may experience if she or he picks up that its interests and skills are gender-inappropriate. The masculine women, the feminine men, need a great deal of confidence, a strong feeling of self-worth and of security, to keep up their battle against traditional sexual expectations; it is no wonder that many men as well as women will avoid this type of conflict or will feel anxious or depressed.

Alfred Adler, the Viennese psychoanalyst, stressed in 1930 that the 'superstition' about women's inferiority has caused enormous damage to the mental development of men and women: 'The thorn of inferiority stings the girl very soon, while the boy is burdened with expectations.'[7]

It is of course possible that some people benefit from adopting the sex-stereotyped role. It may fit them like a glove and, like any glove, provide warmth and security. That of course is fine. There is nothing wrong with the stereotyped model of the feminine woman or the masculine man, apart from the fact that it is a *stereotype*, that is, thought to be applicable to all.

Moving from anecdote to research evidence, I should like to mention a very interesting area of research, research on the terms of masculinity and femininity.[8] When I use these words, I really mean to use them as between quotation marks, for I do not think that we can as yet say what 'masculinity' or 'femininity' really mean. All we know is what has traditionally been seen as masculine and feminine: that there is a traditional agreement on what are feminine personality attributes (i.e. affectionate, warm, dependent, sensitive, caring, etc.) and what are masculine attributes (i.e. independent, assertive, dominant, competitive, forceful, etc.).

Since Freud and Jung there has been a widespread and implicit belief in our culture that the most adjusted unneurotic woman or man possesses to a large degree the attributes which belong to their sex. Certainly, it is also true that both Freud and particularly Jung acknowledge that we all have masculine as well as feminine traits, or *animus* and *anima*. Nevertheless they maintain that too much masculinity in a woman or too much femininity in a man is disastrous. The 'true' woman finds fulfilment in the traditional roles of wife and mother. In taking up a masculine calling, studying and working in a man's way, woman is doing something not wholly in agreement with, if not directly injurious to, her feminine nature, according to Jung. This dichotomous and polarized view of masculinity and femininity has filtered through into much of our thinking. In many cultures, masculine and feminine are used as universal symbols of other dualities: mind-body, passive-active, subjective-objective. Normal men and women had better be at the right end of the pole!

But is this really so? Are the people at each end of the pole particularly healthy and well adjusted? To answer this question a group of men and a group of women were asked to rate themselves on a whole series of attributes, 'masculine, feminine', as well as some more neutral ones.[8,9] On the basis of their ratings it was possible to distinguish between various groups: (i) Men who rated themselves high on masculine and low on feminine attributes, the M+F- (masculine) men; (ii) men who rated themselves low on masculine and high on feminine traits, the M-F+ (feminine) men; (iii) men who rated themselves high on both masculine and feminine attributes, the M+F+ (androgynous) men. Similarly one could distinguish between: (i) the F+M- (feminine); (ii) the F-M+ (masculine); and (iii) the F+M+ (androgynous) women.

Then the same people were given other tests and measures: tests on self esteem, on maturity, adjustment or ego-strength. It appeared that the M+F+ (the androgynous) people - and this was true for both men and women - were significantly the most mature and well adjusted group; that is, those who combine within themselves many attributes, masculine as well as feminine ones, who can be tough as well as tender, passive as well as active, who can lead as well as follow, be independent as well as dependent. The M+F- group of men, the masculine men, were also in fact high on mental health variables. However, in the corresponding F+M- group, the feminine women, high levels of feminine attributes were positively associated with anxiety and negatively with adjustment, ego-strength and autonomy.

You may think that this is common sense, that a person who combines opposing attributes is the healthiest. And if you come to think of it, it *is* - though it is nice that research proves it too. But what is amazing is that our society often assumes exactly the opposite, namely that too many attributes of the other sex do no good.

To summarize this section: there is a need to change, and to change further. There is no justification within psychology for maintaining that men and women are fundamentally and inherently different. There is also no good reason for keeping things as they are, that is, that men and women should to their own benefit remain in different roles. On the contrary, the more we combine in ourselves those attitudes and attributes traditionally seen as feminine and as masculine, the more adjusted and mature a person we are.

If then there is a need for change, away from stereotype and towards fuller maturity, how do we change? I see three factors as important. *First* of all, I think we change through knowledge and through having more information. It is important that opinions are backed by facts. This is one of the reasons why I have here stayed with facts rather than speculation and theories. Knowing more can change our own opinions; it can also help us to change those we talk to. *Secondly*, we change through more or better self-knowledge. I remember an occasion in which a group of clergy wives were asked what model we had had of ourselves as children, as girls, and what expectations we knew our parents had of us. This started us on an analysis of our own development, of our hopes and expectations, our frustrations, and of our endeavours to fit into a mould and our worries if we did not manage it. It helped us to see in what way our early development influenced our later relationships with men and with women. *Thirdly*, we change, we renew ourselves through experience, through the struggles we have gone through and through the people we have met - particularly the people who have ministered to us.

The question of the role of men and women in the Church and of the ordination of women to the priesthood, are questions for the Church to answer. I have taken a step back today and looked at the psychological evidence and I have come to the conclusion that it is not right to use psychological theories in arguments against the ordination of women.

It seems to me that with many people theological reasons given for not ordaining women are connected with emotional reasons: that is, with an individual's feelings and attitudes towards men and women. These attitudes themselves have been formed and moulded from early infancy onwards, particularly by our parents. I do not mean to say that all theological arguments against the ordination of women are inspired by the attitudes towards men and women of the people who hold them. I only suggest that the readiness with which people turn to them, or the priority they give to such arguments has a lot to do with their own psychological make-up. That is why I am hopeful. Views on issues which have a strong emotional undertone, like the question of the ordination of women, often change slowly. Change after all can be very uncomfortable, particularly if so much of ourselves is invested in our views. But views *do* change, if there is more knowledge, better self-understanding and through new relationships. And if there is change and renewal, it will go, I am convinced, in the direction of a more balanced partnership of men and women in the life of the churches, so using the gifts of the whole of humanity.

Notes

1. M.S. Horner, 'Motive to Avoid Success and Changing Aspirations of Women'. in J. Bardwick (ed.), *Readings on the Psychology of Women*, New York, Harper and Row, 1972.

2. M. Carlsson and P. Jäderquist, 'Note on Sex-role Opinions as Conceptual Schemata' (*British J.Soc.Psych.*, 22, 1983), pp. 65-8.

3. D.M. Broverman, *et al.*, *Sex-role Stereotypes and Clinical Judgements of Mental Health*, New York, Basic Books, 1981.

4. For a review and discussion of the issue of sex differences, see E.E. Maccoby and C.N. Jacklin, *The Psychology of Sex Differences*, California, Stanford University Press, 1974.

5. D. Griffith and E. Saraga, 'Sex Differences in Cognitive Abilities: a Sterile Field of Enquiry?' in O. Hartnett, G. Boden, M. Fuller (eds.), *Women: Sex-role Stereotyping*, Tavistock Publications, 1979.

6. H. Frish, 'Sex Stereotypes in Adult-Infant Play' (*Child Development*, 48, 1977), pp. 1671-5.

7. A. Adler, *The Education of Children*, Allen and Unwin, 1930.

8. S.L. Bem, 'On the Utility of Alternative Procedures for Assessing Psychological Androgyny' (*J. of Cons. and Clin. Psych.*, US, 1977), pp. 196-205.

9. J.A. Williams, 'Psychological Androgyny and Mental Health', in O. Hartnett, G. Boden, M. Fuller (eds.), op. cit.

TEN

Called to Priesthood:
Interpreting Women's Experience

Mary Tanner

Contemporary puzzles of Church order and morals cannot be solved simply by referring to words or customs of the past. Neither the hallowed words of Scripture nor the treasured words of the Church's tradition can, on their own, determine the hard question of the ordination of women to the priesthood.

> Religion, like everything else under the moon, continually changes, continually requires to be adjusted, re-examined, reformed, interpreted anew 'as it is by change and nature's changing course untrimmed'. In periods of slow change, this necessity is felt more gradually; in periods of rapid change like ours, the necessity is more obvious and pressing. But religion never stands still.[1]

The Holy Spirit in the midst of us and ahead of us is always challenging us to take a fresh look at what God has entrusted to his Church in Scripture and tradition. It is in an interplay of Scripture and tradition, reason and experience, that we renegotiate inherited doctrines and beliefs. This is what makes the Christian way very exciting, unexpected and always re-creative. In the dance between what we have inherited and what we experience, we as individuals and the Church as the Body of Christ are led to new insights. Scripture sometimes marvellously confirms lived experience, says 'yes' to what is new and radical. Equally we may not deny its power to judge and condemn our experience; it can and does sometimes say 'no' to change.

This double dynamic process is being affirmed by more and more theologians who acknowledge that the experience of individuals and communities is a valid subject for reflection in theological endeavour. Careful attention to the way things function and the way things are is an essential part of 'doing theology'. They claim, with Bonhoeffer, the importance of 'never understanding the reality of God apart from the reality of the world'. God's word is heard, his demands perceived in a disturbing and creative interaction between what is going on in the world and what has so far been understood, believed and practised in the Christian tradition. This way of 'doing theology' is not new. It is the pattern described in contemporary biblical scholarship as the dynamic behind the canonical revelation. Prophets, wisdom writers, psalmists, gospel writers pondered on the traditions they had inherited in the light of their contemporary experience, both personal and national. With astonishing openness to the life-giving tradition, carried in their Scriptures and encountered in their worship, with openness to social and religious life and to personal relationships, and above all with an openness to the power of the Spirit, they were led to see new truths about the nature and being of God, to perceive new things about their relationship to God and to each other and were able to proclaim a vision for the present and the immediate future. The tradition passed on both within Scripture and outside is thus dynamic and not static. Development is part of the biblical and Christian way.

Nowhere is this theological process, with its emphasis on experience, welcomed and more eagerly explored today than among women. For so long the silent ones in forming the tradition, in passing it down, in interpreting it officially, women are discovering a new confidence in 'doing theology'. They are beginning to tell their stories and share their experience, and they are examining Scripture and tradition in the light of this newly found confidence in their experience. 'Women's experience' is for some an ambiguous and impenetrable phrase. As Nicola Slee points out in a fascinating article, 'Parables and Women's Experience', the term 'women's experience' does raise questions about gender differentiation and its relation to biological and social factors, the cultural and historical context of experience and so on. Nevertheless the term is, as she suggests, a convenient shorthand device for pointing to those aspects of women's lives which are unique to them by virtue of being women and which have been silenced for so long. Without denying the radically different manifestations of women's experience, according to their different circumstances, cultural and economic and social, Nicola Slee argues that

> there remains an underlying unity of experience forged by women's common physiological nature and by a shared history and present experience of oppression and powerlessness. Within the terms of such analysis, to speak of 'women's experience' serves the dual function of both affirming that common reality of experience and attempting to redress the imbalance perpetuated by a system in which the dominant forms of thought and expression are determined by and reflect the needs of the socially powerful gender group and where, consequently, the needs and experiences of women are forgotten, ignored, or, at best, subsumed under categories created by and appropriate to men.[2]

It is this experience of women which is being written about and shared more confidently that must be brought into the debate on the ordination of women to the priesthood. Many women as well as men see this emphasis on experience as a threat. They interpret the offering of 'women's experience' as part of the theological task as an emotional attempt to overturn the old, to substitute something different and to make an unacceptable break in continuity with the past. But in bringing their experience into dialogue with Scripture and tradition, in attempting to make sense of their experience in the light of what they have inherited, women are not seeking to destroy the tradition but rather to discover a fuller, richer truth cradled in what the Church has safeguarded. Those richer things are there to be set free by the key of experience.

It is on the basis of this theological methodology, with its dynamic holistic approach, that the Church of England needs to set about discovering the truth about women and priesthood. The case for or against cannot be decided by balancing two sets of arguments from Scripture and tradition, one for, the other against, and watching to see which way the scales tip. The task of theology, under the guidance of the Spirit, is more fascinating, more exciting than this. There is new evidence in the

1980s which we have to make room for. We need to listen to what women and men are claiming the Spirit is saying in and through contemporary experience. The stories of women, particularly of women in ministry, are the 'algebraic signs' for the community, gifts to be used and interpreted as we wrestle with the puzzle of women and priesthood and seek to form the mind of the Church. There is a great deal in the stories women are telling that deserves to be considered. But one feature in particular that demands careful attention is what women, and not only women but whole communities, are claiming about God's call to priesthood. This is so often brushed aside as irrelevant, subjective evidence. Women who claim a call to priesthood are dismissed as misguided, deluded, arrogant, status-seeking. How can women receive a call to priesthood when the Church does not provide for the testing of such a call? It is implied that no call can be received as long as the institutional Church makes no provision for testing it.

But surely to dismiss the testimony from a growing number of women to be called by God to a priestly ministry is to do less than justice to the Church tradition itself. The God whom Christians claim to have faith in is a creator God who does not remain remote from that which he has created but moves always towards his creations in love. He is a God who from the earliest time, from the patriarch Abraham, takes the initiative and calls men and women into relation with himself. He calls them to serve him and to serve one another in him. Indeed, every Christian baptized into the death of Christ rises through the waters of baptism and is called to a life of service. We acknowledge and say 'yes' to that call in confirmation, and reaffirm our response at every Eucharist. Christian discipleship is one of responding to a call from God. To be a Christian is to know that it belongs to the nature of God that he calls us out of the world to serve him.

We know too that God calls to special ministries and functions and gives special grace to men and women to respond. Even if we have not experienced this as individuals, it is so much a part of the Christian story that we encounter in Scripture and in the testimony of Christians through the ages. Within the Bible we see this confirmed again and again in the stories of the prophets. One after another they testify to an overwhelming sense of the call of Yahweh. No two calls are experienced in the same way, and yet the realization of a power outside themselves, beckoning and calling for a special task, is common to each of the prophets. Amos feels called by God from following the sheep and directed to a ministry in the northern kingdom; Isaiah hears, through the words of the liturgy of the Temple, the voice of God saying, 'Whom shall I send, and who will go for us?'; Ezekiel is overpowered by the Spirit of God, feels the 'hand of God' grasping him and is aware of God calling; and Jeremiah, more than any of the prophets, witnesses again and again to the power of God's call and, although he is called to a ministry of isolation and suffering, he cannot shut out the voice of the Lord. For women, the call of Mary, the most incredible and astonishing call of all, shows that God is a God who calls to the unthinkable, to that which is beyond belief. As the Old Testament prophets responded to their calls, and as Mary responded in obedience to her call, the response meant becoming vulnerable and facing rejection and humiliation.

Why is it, that born within such a tradition, women who claim to have been called by God to a vocation of priesthood, are regarded with so much suspicion? Surely they deserve at least a sympathetic hearing from those who believe in a God who calls. After all it is hard to admit publicly a belief to be called by God to a vocation which is denied by the institutional Church. Only a woman who is very convinced of her call will find the strength to confess that publicly. One of the first women to be ordained to the priesthood in America, the Reverend Carter Heyward, describes that particular experience of pain at going against the Church in her book, *A Priest Forever*.

> In a society and in a Church in which woman has been put into a place out of which she cannot move, any effort on her part to burst out of this place will be considered strange or abnormal. Those invested with institutional authority are likely to get their backs up and balk defensively at her efforts. For such a woman is a threat both to men and woman who have heavy investment in maintaining the present order.[3]

Elizabeth Canham, an English woman, who in 1981 was

ordained a priest in America, echoes Carter Hayward's words in the telling of her story, her 'pilgrimage to priesthood'. Of the time when, after ordination as a deaconess in Southwark Cathedral, she became convinced of a vocation to priesthood, she writes:

> I knew that I was going to have to live with tension whatever the outcome, for though the diaconate was a step towards my vocation, I would be suspended for years at least in this interim state, and I did not feel it was my ultimate goal. Moreover, I knew that the more articulate I became, the more of a threat I would pose to those who were not ready to consider that women might become priests.[4]

No woman without an overwhelming sense of a call from outside herself would willingly embrace the isolation and pain that comes with confessing she believes she is called to priesthood. Many women tell of trying to shut out such a call, to turn their backs on it, as Jeremiah tried to turn his back on his call to be a prophet. Many, like him, find they can do no other than be faithful to their call whatever that brings. To deny the call would be to deny the voice of God; to respond to the call is to be divided sometimes from colleagues and close friends and to be rejected by the Church.

As we listen to the stories women are telling, we find that hardly ever is the call received in a blinding flash. It is not like Paul's sudden and dramatic experience on the Damascus road. Rather, it is a sense of awareness which grows slowly and painfully, often against all that is expected or hoped for. The following story is a very typical one of how women grow in an awareness that God is calling them to a ministry they can only recognize as a priestly ministry.

> Already as a young teenager, I began to wonder if God was calling me to some form of Christian ministry. The idea certainly did not attract me. Nevertheless, a year or so later, I can remember preaching imaginary sermons. I never shared any of this with anyone at the time. Women didn't preach sermons in those days and I certainly didn't want to be thought odd!

155

As I grew up this unwelcome sense of call stayed with me. I trained as a secretary and worked for a major publishing company, where I soon had opportunities to do editing and to write. I attended a large evangelical Church and was confirmed. This church laid great stress on Christian vocation. I knew little of the full-time ministry open to women in the Church of England at that time. It seemed to me that the only course of action open to me as a woman would be in missionary work. The picture would, I believe, have looked far different if women could have been priests. After five and a half years in publishing and another two at the BBC, I went to Germany to work as a secretary for two years. The sense of God's call had become far less unwelcome by this time and I think I already knew when I left for Germany that I would return to prepare for some form of full-time Christian service. I did not know what this would be.

Gill Cooke continues to tell how she returned to England, read theology and planned to work for a missionary society, but found in the routine office work they directed her towards, she could not use her theological training or linguistic expertise, and so, disappointed, she returned to the BBC. She continues:

> I went back to work as a secretary at the BBC, but I felt completely shattered. My faith was central to my life, and I had followed where I felt God was calling me, and now . . . On the secular side I received every encouragement. I was offered very good jobs. But I still felt God's call to me was to ministry. I gradually began to wonder if I was mistaken. I discussed my feelings about ministry with the Rector at the Church I attended. I said something about preaching and was told very firmly God did not intend women to preach. He told me instead how much God had blessed his secretary in her vocation.

Gill's story tells how with little encouragement and certainly no fostering of her vocation by the clergy and with no role-models of women in ministry to follow, two years later she went to theological college and entered parochial work and undertook a part-time chaplaincy post in a polytechnic. After a period of three years the bishop asked her to become minister-in-charge of a parish while continuing in the chaplaincy. She carries on her story:

> As minister-in-charge I had the same responsibilities as any vicar, but had always to make sure what I did was legal! I could baptise, preach, take funerals, but could not celebrate the Eucharist nor marry couples. As president of this worshipping community most regular communicants preferred to have me preside and give communion from the reserved sacrament, than to have a priest come in from outside, who they did not know, to celebrate . . .
>
> After five and a half years of professional lay ministry in the Church of England I find my views have changed considerably. When I began, I refused to answer when anyone asked whether I felt called to the priesthood; the opportunity was not there and so I claimed the question was a non-question. But throughout my ministry I have become aware that my ministry is hampered because I cannot be ordained. Because I cannot celebrate, I must always invite someone in to do so, and that person may have no understanding of the needs of the group or the church. Many times I have prepared couples for marriage, but could not take the ceremony although in some cases it was particularly important to them that I did so. I have, in the course of counselling, heard many confessions, but although I can pray with and reassure people of God's forgiveness, I am not able to give formal absolution.

Gill's account is one that is echoed again and again in the stories women tell. It is of a growing, often unwelcome conviction: that of God's call to ministry and, more than that, to a specifically priestly ministry. It is usually quite unexpected, against all the patterns of ministry with which the women were familiar. With no role-models to stimulate the desire for such a ministry, this awareness and conviction of a growing number of women is not easy to explain away. What is more, the lack of enthusiasm and encouragement given to women, particularly from male priests, in contrast to the fostering of vocations in men, makes the determination to respond to God's call even more impressive.

Frances Briscoe, now a deaconess, previously a school teacher, begins her story like this:

> 'Don't do it! Don't do it! Don't do it!'

This was the reaction which met my first tentative inquiries regarding full-time ministry in the Church of England.

'You'll die of frustration,' said one.
'Your gifts will be stifled,' commented another.
'Stay in teaching,' advised a third.

At the time I was responsible for the teaching of Religious Education in a large, mixed secondary modern school. It was a challenging and stimulating job, which I enjoyed. When I told my vicar I thought God was calling me to the Church he did his utmost to dissuade me - on the grounds of the valuable job I was doing in the local school. Subsequently I discussed my 'call' with a former parish worker, and a deaconess who visited the parish. These were the only two women in ministry I had met. Both gravely warned me I might regret leaving teaching for the Church.

No role-models again, no encouragement, indeed positive discouragement, from the church leaders; and yet, convinced of her call, Frances responded, becoming first a lay minister, and later a deaconess.

Like any other candidate for the diaconate - deacon or deaconess - I was asked by the bishop:

'Do you trust that you are inwardly moved by the Holy Spirit to take upon you the office and ministration . . .?'

I was able to reply, 'I trust so,' with confidence because of my own inner conviction. But more than this my inner conviction of a call had been ratified by the way my ministry had been accepted in the parish. For me this indicated a divine seal of approval, which was visibly demonstrated in the Cathedral that day by the presence of over 200 people from the parish. Never have I been so conscious of such love and prayerful support.

God calls; the Spirit equips. This is true for both men and women. As it is so, ought not the threefold ministry of the church to be open to both men and women who feel called and are manifestly so equipped?

This last thought in Frances's story adds another fact which recurs in the stories women are telling about their journey

towards the priestly ministry. It is not often that the call comes
in an experience of God speaking directly to them. Rather it is a
call which comes through others. The community calls forth
gifts of women, gifts they themselves were not aware they had
to offer. So often the community confirms what women
themselves are too hesitant, too fearful to acknowledge. This
way of God's call confirms God's way in history. God works
both in calling individuals but also through communities which
ask and draw out gifts in individuals.

One of the most impressive stories of a call coming from a
community is written by Peggy Hartley about her experience of
being called. It came late in life as she neared retirement:

A telephone call from a churchwarden of a parish in which I used to
live led me to consider, for the first time, the possibility of full-time
ministry in a parish. Having spent twenty-five years in church
social work, ten of them in teaching pastoralia in a theological
college, I had come to the decision that it was time I returned to
social work of some kind, for my last few years of work before
retirement.

Then came the question: 'A few of us have been discussing
whether it would be possible for you to come here as our minister.
What do you think?' My response was that such things did not
happen in the Church of England, to a laywoman. I almost
dismissed the telephone call, but not quite, a seed had been sown.
The question came again, this time from the vicar who was leaving.
We both knew that it could not be thought about further until the
bishop had been approached.

Meanwhile I applied for a social work post that I felt drawn to,
only to meet the bishop the next day and to be told that he had
received a letter from some members of the Parish Church Council
with a request that they would like the possibility of my being their
minister to be considered. The bishop made inquiries, first of all by
seeing representatives from the parish, and then by meeting all the
PCC. He was satisfied that the PCC would welcome the
appointment, and that they felt it would be acceptable to other
parishioners. It was then that I felt able to consider it seriously, and
as I talked with the bishop, my whole being assented to such a
ministry. As I look back over my life I am so conscious that all I

have done before and all that has happened to me in happiness and in pain, has prepared me for this ministry. It was no thought of mine. I believe it has to come from the heart of love, at the centre of life that we name God and it has brought me a task and a fulfilment for which I continually give thanks.

After a description of her work in the parish, which differs little from that of any parish priest, Peggy writes:

I sincerely believe that women should be ordained, but I cannot believe that I would feel any different or more open as a channel for the Holy Spirit if I could say certain prayers and perform certain actions. I feel ordained now – as one of the parishioners wrote to me last Christmas: 'While the Church argues whether women should or should not be ordained, it has already happened in this parish.' It is felt by others, I feel it too. The ordination of women has much opposition which hides a lot of anger and aggression, I believe, having its roots deep in our experience of sexuality, and our belief in God. We must not fight with anger or prejudice other people's deep feelings. We take the hurt that comes through the denial of our recognition by the Church of England and go on ministering in love, speaking and working for the truth as we see it, in love. In these ways we may be instruments in bringing new life into our Church and in our Christian communities.

These stories contain their own power. They are not about militant, strident women claiming their rights, equal rights with men in the public institution of the Church. They are stories of women, who against all the odds, have experienced slowly, and often painfully and fearfully, a growing sense that God is calling them to ministry. Often the call is interpreted in the only way the Church makes possible, as a call to lay ministry. Often it is only after responding to that, after ministering to communities as lay women, that the call comes to be understood as a call to a full sacramental priestly ministry. This is never talked of with pride, hardly ever with anger that the call cannot be answered. Rather it is told with amazement that God should, through others, be asking of them a priestly ministry.

There is another side to these stories which reflects and

confirms the experience of the women. This is echoed in the stories told by those who receive the ministry of women. We heard it in the comment of a parishioner: 'While the Church argues whether women should or should not be ordained, it has already happened in this parish.' I am reminded of the occasion when a parish priest of Catholic persuasion spoke of his experience of working with a parish worker. When she joined his staff he was opposed to the opening of the priesthood to women. The woman herself felt no call to priesthood. Her lay ministry and his priestly ministry were to complement each other and to satisfy both and form the basis of their partnership. But after three years of working closely together, he bowed to what he saw God doing in and through her ministry. The only judgement he found himself able to make, in spite of his earlier firmly held convictions, was 'she is already a priest'. And so it is not only the women who grow in understanding their call to priesthood, but others who, changed by the experience of women in ministry, are led to affirm that God is indeed calling women to something new.

It is stories such as these that have to be told and listened to in the search for an answer, God's answer, to this hard question of the ordination of women to the priesthood. This experience must be brought into dialogue with Scripture and tradition. What can we make of such experience in the light of the Church's tradition, and how does this experience in its turn help us to interpret Scripture and tradition? We must ask what it means that women feel called to a full sacramental ministry, that communities are calling forth priestly gifts from more and more women, and what it means that a growing number of people from all wings of the Church are recognizing that it is so. We have to consider what such signs of new life mean in the context of a religion that believes in a God who is there ahead of us, leading us into new understandings; what it means that women feel called to priesthood in the context of a religion that believes in a God who calls individuals to astonishingly new ministries, a God who often calls through the needs of communities.

It is in the interaction of what we make of these contemporary stories, and what we make of the Christian story, that we shall be led to truth. God's word is heard, his guidance found in the creative interaction between what is going on in the Church and the world and what has so far been understood, believed and practised in the Church tradition.

Notes

1. Richard Hanson, 'Sweet Illusion of the Good Old Faith', *The Times*, 25 February 1984.

2. Nicola Slee, 'Parables and Women's Experience', *The Modern Churchman*, XXVI, 2, 1984.

3. Carter Heyward, *A Priest Forever* (New York, Harper and Row, 1976), p. 32.

4. Elizabeth Canham, *Pilgrimage to Priesthood*, SPCK, 1983.

ELEVEN

The Right Time*

John Austin Baker

The Bible makes a lot of use of the idea of right, appropriate or
critical time. Does this offer us any help in making up our
minds whether or not this is the right moment to press ahead
for any particular goal? Or, more generally, does it provide any
broad principles for discerning any 'right time' from a 'wrong
time' on any matter? For reasons which will appear, I do not
think the Bible does or indeed can answer that sort of question,
that is, I do not think that what the Bible says about particular
critical times, or the way it uses the idea of 'right time', can ever
give us techniques for discerning the next 'right time' or
arguments for showing when it has really arrived. The decision
on that point has to be taken in faith. That does not mean that
our study will be wasted. Quite the contrary. But it does mean
that we shall be disappointed if we expect too much, or the
wrong sort of results from it.

The scholarly background to our study has two main
elements. The first, and most controversial, is that of the
Hebrew and Greek notions of time. Did the Old Testament
have a different idea of time from that current in the world of
the New Testament? And if so, were the New Testament
writers more influenced by this Old Testament concept than by
the ideas taken for granted by their contemporaries in the
pagan culture of the Mediterranean Graeco-Roman society?
The second, more straightforward question, is linked with the
first and concerns two Greek words for 'time' used in the New
Testament, viz. *kairos* and *khronos*. The latter, *khronos*, is
familiar to all of us in such words as 'chronicle', 'chronic', and
has the simple, predominant sense 'elapsed time' - so many
hours, days, years, centuries. The other word, *kairos*, has given

---

*First published as a pamphlet by the Movement for the Ordination of Women.

us no English terms, but it is this from which our subject of the 'right' or 'critical' time derives, so it will be as well to start by saying something about this.

Kairos in Greek probably has as its basic meaning something like 'due', 'fitting', 'appropriate', 'in right proportion' – that is to say, in the most general way, what is right in the given circumstances. A line by the early Greek poet, Hesiod, became a proverb and indeed expresses a very deep conviction of the Greek spirit: 'In everything the appropriate (*kairos*) is best.' Xenophon writes of someone's stomach being 'greater than was proper (*kairos*)'. The word could also be used of the real point in an argument, the crucial issue. It is, so to speak, the bull's-eye you need to hit in order to be right, and its exact reference is then determined by the context.

But the main area in which the word was used came to be that of 'time'. As you would expect, one of its principal meanings in that context was, of course, the 'right' or 'critical' time, what we might call the 'timely' time. Some phrases vividly display the differences between *kairos* and *khronos*. Hippocrates, the great medical writer, speaks of the '*kairos* in which there is not much *khronos*', the critical opportunity, in other words, which does not last very long. The Greeks talked of a word or action being 'in *kairos*', where we would say 'in season', 'before the *kairos*' meaning 'premature', and so on. In the end, however, by a process we find in all languages as they get old, tired and lazy, these crisp and vivid distinctions, which depend so much on care and precision in the use of words, faded away, and *kairos* came to be used indifferently for all the senses in which we use the word 'time' – even, in the plural, in the same way as we talk about 'the times' being hard or out of joint.

Nevertheless, Greek did have this very useful word which never quite lost the sense of 'the right time', 'the crucial moment'. And so we find it in the New Testament. A few examples must stand for many possible ones. Thus in Matthew the demons ask Jesus, 'Have you come here to torment us before the *kairos*?', that is, the fore-ordained and legitimate moment of the Last Judgement. Again, when Jesus sends the disciples into Jerusalem to prepare the upper room for the Last Supper, the message he gives them is: 'The Master says, My *kairos* is near.' In Luke he weeps over Jerusalem, saying, 'You did not know the *kairos* of your visitation.' Turning to the Epistles we find St Paul in Romans, for example, saying that 'Christ died for the ungodly in accordance with the *kairos*,' at the right or proper time. When writing to the Corinthians about the collection for the famine-stricken Christians at Jerusalem, he talks about 'your surplus being applied to their lack at this present *kairos*' – this is the moment when the money is needed, not next month or next year, so stop messing about.

As I say, one could multiply examples, but I am sure by now the point has been made. So let me take the argument on a bit further by giving you two slightly more complex cases. The first comes from St John's Gospel. In chapter 7 Jesus says to his family: 'My *kairos* is not yet here; but your *kairos* is always ready.' There is something really rather important here. For a worldly person, someone who thinks in purely human and expedient terms, any moment may be the right one, any moment can be exploited to their advantage. But for someone whose meat and drink is to do the will of God the decision is not their own to make; they must wait for *God's* moment. In this case it involves Jesus in apparent equivocation. The same idea from a rather different standpoint is found in Mark 1.15, the message Jesus is said to have proclaimed at the very start of his public ministry: 'The *kairos* is fulfilled, and the Kingdom of God has arrived; repent and believe the Good News.' The *kairos* is fulfilled, literally 'the *kairos* has been completed, has reached the moment of fulness,' or, as we might say 'the time is ripe'. Here again we have the sense of waiting for some moment dictated by a power or authority outside ourselves. In this case the process of fulfilment in mind is the whole history of Israel, which has been leading up to this moment. At last everything is falling into place; God's grand design has reached its denouement. It is D-Day: the invasion of this world by the sovereign power of God is beginning, so recognize the fact, turn from your neglect of God and acknowledge this message of joy and victory.

In both cases we have this fundamental new consideration, that the 'right moment' is not a matter of simply being clever enough to catch the tide or exploit an opening but of recognizing the opportunity that God has deliberately created for this particular purpose. So indeed our topic is highly relevant to the question about the ordination of women. *Is* this the opportunity God has deliberately created for this new development in the life of Christ's Church?

This particular usage in the New Testament is indeed intimately related to the Old Testament background. The very idea of divine purpose, of a plan unfolding stage by stage is fundamental to the great majority of the Old Testament writers. To take but one example of the idea of a number of factors converging to bring in God's D-Day, God tells Abraham in Genesis that his descendants will have to be enslaved in a foreign land for 400 years before they can occupy the Promised Land, because they cannot be allowed to invade and conquer it until the wickedness of the inhabitants has become great enough to merit that punishment. Or, to turn to quite a different writer, Isaiah constantly refers to the secret plan of Yahweh, which to human eyes seems totally baffling; it is a 'strange', or 'alien deed', because human minds cannot follow its reason or sequence. Again, much later, the whole of apocalyptic literature, beginning with the Book of Daniel, is based on the belief that God has a predestined scheme, so tightly planned that to those specially favoured can be revealed even the precise number of years each stage will take. The end of such a process is precisely what the New Testament means by the *kairos*.

This fits in with another Old Testament motif, that of the Day of the Lord, or as it is sometimes called, simply '*the* Day' or '*that* Day'. Amos makes it clear that the real Day of Yahweh can be known only to God's servants the prophets whose whole being is open to the divine message. The ordinary Israelites, heedless of God's law or spirit, immersed in their egotistical human plans and desires, say they want the Day of the Lord, because they think of God as someone who will obligingly intervene to use miraculous power to give them what *they* want. God will indeed intervene, Amos says, but only at the moment which fits the divine plan, and to do what is right in the eyes of divine justice - which will not suit them at all: 'Why do you desire the Day of the Lord? It is darkness, and not light.'

The Old Testament, then, contains as a prominent and formative feature of its thought the idea of historic time as a purposeful process, and of particular moments within that process as being critical points at which God's purposes are advanced or fulfilled by unique acts of intervention. The process need not be a single line. As I have already instanced (and I could easily have given other examples) it may be a convergence of several lines, the completion of a pattern. But the 'Days of the Lord', the moments of special divine intervention, have two functions in relation to these processes. They bring one phase to completion; and they set in motion another. Thus the destruction of Jerusalem in 586 brought one whole story to an end; but it also started another, the birth of Judaism as a religious rather than a political system. The prophetic longing for *the* Day of the Lord', the decisive and climactic Day, is to be understood as a desire for the completion of the total cosmic process, the end not of a chapter but of the whole universal book, when everyone, or at any rate the righteous, would live happily ever after. In primitive Christianity this took the form of interpreting Jesus, especially in the light of his resurrection, as the one who had ushered in this final Day of the Lord, so that the end of the world could confidently be expected at any moment. But, of course, this turned out to be a wrong interpretation. Jesus was the beginning of yet another chapter; and the Church has never really cleared its mind as to whether or in what sense that chapter is to be the last.

I would now like to pursue these general biblical ideas in the context of our special concern. The first point I want to underline is that 'the right time', in biblical thought, is not 'the *opportune* moment' but 'the *God-given* moment'. The Bible does not see these *kairoi*, these critical junctures, simply as openings that occur in the evolutionary march of history and which some people are ready to exploit. It is not even a question of God inspiring people to exploit these opportunities when they arise. It is a matter of God actually creating the pregnant or opportune situation.

Now, taking that a bit further, we have to say that the 'opportunities' which God creates, and which are indeed the crucial openings for the divine purposes, often do not look a bit like an opportunity to most people, or perhaps look like an opportunity for something quite different, which God did not have in mind at all. The supreme example here, of course, is Christ himself. Quite a lot of people thought that Jesus was a God-sent opening, a *kairos*, but for what? Not for what Jesus had in mind, or God. The real purposes (some of them anyway, for I am sure we are still far from understanding all the purposes God had and has in mind in Jesus) only became apparent after the resurrection, and then only bit by bit as various people, such as Paul and John, read some of them off. The New Testament itself applies this idea, of people's failure to see what God is really at, to the Old Testament. In fact you could say that the separate identity of Christianity, as distinct from Judaism, depended on Christians proving, at least to the satisfaction of some, that Israel had consistently got it wrong, and had used the God-given *kairoi* for the wrong purposes. Stephen's speech to the Sanhedrin in Acts 7 is a classic example of this. What is the *kairos* for? That is one key question; and all one can perhaps say is that the right answer will be generally in line with the character and priorities of Jesus, that is, it will be in tune with his mind and spirit.

There is, indeed, another very possible reaction to a *kairos*, and that is not to see it as particularly significant in any way. The majority of Jews quite sincerely did not see Jesus or his followers as marking any sort of God-given moment. Whether you recognize a *kairos* when it comes must depend, in the first instance, on what you already think about God and the kind of things that God might conceivably be concerned to do.

Another fairly basic question to be asked about God's *kairoi* is: how are they brought about? Through what agency do the lines converge and is the pattern brought to temporary completion? To this the Bible offers no single answer, precisely because each *kairos* is the result of a number of different factors and different kinds of factor.

What I mean is this. The development of what we call 'secular' thought or culture is not to be dismissed as no part either of God's preparation of a *kairos* or of the interpretation that divine love and wisdom want us to put upon it. The Bible will not allow us to draw any such pious conclusion. A major creative element in patriarchal religion, and so in the whole conception of God's relation to a human family, was the personal clan or tribal deity in a special relationship with the clan chieftain in Aramean society. Some of the most fruitful ingredients in the early Old Testament laws were borrowed straight from Hurrian codes. Israel would never have gone over to kingship when it did simply on its own initiative – monarchy was an invention of the pagan world and Israel was merely conforming to that world, much to the anxiety and distaste of many of its finest spiritual leaders at the time – but, equally clearly, kingship did introduce new ideas vitally needed, whose course is not yet run, not to mention the title of 'Christ' itself. In prophecy, worship, wisdom and every other Old Testament sphere the story is the same. And it continues in the New Testament. The New Testament writers, so far from being suspicious of contemporary secular ideas, take them over, use them, develop them. Their cry is not, 'We are utterly different from you', but 'We can beat you at your own game'. They quote the ideals of social and individual behaviour taught in popular Stoic education, and simply urge Christians to show that they can do all that and more. They borrow the salvation-thinking of the mysteries, and say, 'We can actually deliver these goods, because *our* Saviour-Hero was a real man who genuinely did die and rise again.' The fact that we may now be doubtful of the validity of some of the ideas they did take over and use does not prove that Christians ought never to contemplate using *any* secular ideas or values. At every stage of the divine plan for human redemption and maturity the world has been laid under contribution both as a source of inspiration and as a means of communication; and, so far as the Bible is concerned, this has been God's intention, and the results, sometimes for a purely limited period, sometimes more permanently, have set forward his kingdom.

In my judgement, therefore, it would be quite impossible, on biblical grounds, to argue that because 'equality for women' or 'the liberation of women' (or whatever label for the sexual revolution is least misleading) is a fashionable cause in secular circles it is something Christians should either deeply suspect or even avoid on principle. On the contrary, its presence in the secular world could well, on biblical precedent, be a creative factor preparing a divine *kairos*. And surely this must be so, because, if there is one thing the Bible makes clearer than any other, it is that all God's plans are aimed at the ultimate good of the whole creation, not just of the particular group who may be the chosen agents of the redemptive programme at any given time. Israel, at least in the mainstream of Old Testament and Judaistic thought, exists for the sake of the nations. The Church in the New Testament exists, at least in its primal commission, for the sake of the world. It was for the sake of the world that God gave the Redeemer, that God was in Christ. So every divine *kairos* is going to be 'the right time' to achieve or attempt something for the world. Whatever happens in the Church ought to be judged by that criterion. It would, therefore, be reasonable to say, 'We will not take this step, because we believe it will encourage developments in the world which are not what God wills for the human race as a whole.' It is not reasonable nor biblical to say, 'We will not take this step because it would be very like current developments in the world.' To reject something *just because* it is also a contemporary secular belief or value is alien to the whole biblical ethos, the weight of which cannot be offset by quoting isolated texts.

There is, however, the other element in the preparation and exploitation of a divine *kairos*, and that is the prophetic witness and interpretation. And here we come back to the question I raised earlier on: What is the *kairos* for? For what divine leap forward is this 'the right time'? I do not see how we can generalize about this except to say that, as I mentioned just now, the new development must presumably be in harmony with the mind and spirit of Christ. In our particular concern this test has usually been applied by asking what were the attitudes to women which we find in the gospel picture of Jesus or implicit in the theology of the New Testament Church. The arguments, however, are, as one might expect, quite inconclusive. There is general agreement that Jesus was more liberal in his dealings with women than Judaism at that time officially approved, though Vermes has given some reason to believe that in charismatic circles in Galilee the rather narrow rules taught by some rabbis were already disregarded. It is accepted that he accorded them greater spiritual equality than most of his contemporaries. On the other hand, some will argue, he did not give any official commission or authority to any woman; and for those who identify 'apostleship' with 'ordination' (a very dubious equation) this is naturally decisive. Others would argue, again with considerable scholarly support, that Jesus never thought in terms of a church and ordination anyway, so how can one validly argue from his practice, whatever it was, to our situation? As for the witness of the Acts and Epistles, it is hard to find any relevant attitude there on which all writers are agreed. Arguments tend to be highly selective, and to assume that the most inspired bits are those which appeal to modern thought. St Paul is reflecting the Spirit when he says that in Christ there is neither male nor female, but obviously unregenerate when he rules, 'Let a woman keep silence in the congregation'. Not unnaturally there are those who give the opposite assessment of the same passages.

The assumption behind this sort of debate is, I believe, that the point of the *kairos* we are at is, first, to develop the role of women in the Church, and secondly, to decide whether or not this includes certainly priestly activities. Both sides would agree that God is calling us to a more balanced and fuller human partnership in which women have an equal share with men, and contribute their complementary gifts to the whole. On that point they agree that this is a *kairos*, and that we must respond to it. Where they disagree, as we all know, is whether an equal share means that everything men do women shall be allowed to do also. It is a little difficult to exclude men from something that women are allowed to do in the Church, because there is no ecclesiastical function women have that men do not have already. (A pity because it leaves that side of the case with a burden of seeming inequity to carry which has to be relieved by elaborate and not very convincing theological arguments!) What I want to ask is this. Have those who debate along these lines really understood what the present *kairos* is for? What is this 'the right time' for? What pattern is nearing completion? What actions are we called upon to take to complete it, and to initiate the next part of the design? What ideas abroad in the world are really speaking to us with the voice of God? And how does God's spirit want us to respond to them for the good of the whole human family? It may well be, as I see it, that the real questions being asked in the world today, the fundamental ideas being developed, are not about anything so specific as the role of the sexes, but about peaceful coexistence, about the nature of authority, of community, of moral sanctions, of coping with knowledge and power without either tyrannizing over the individual or letting the collective racket itself to pieces. These are the deepest issues behind the clash between Marxist and capitalist, totalitarian and democratic societies, between institutional religion and individual spiritualities, and so forth. At the same time the whole unfinished secularization debate is asking the Church: How are you related to the world? What does incarnation mean for church structures and mission in this regard? What ought Christians to be promoting in the great issues I have mentioned for the good of all humankind, and how do they go about it? Do they get dissolved into the body politic, and, if so, how? Do they in their own affairs (which there must inevitably be) develop models which might be helpful in a wider context?

If I am right, and these are the challenges facing the human race today - crucial challenges which may destroy us if we cannot answer them - then the question God is asking the Church, the *kairos* we are being offered, is not so much about whether women should be admitted to the ordained ministry, it is about the very nature and function, perhaps the very existence of ministry itself. If the Church is to develop models of its own life, which are expressive of God's identification with us in Christ, and that genuine identification of the strong with the weak, of the rich with the poor, which must be our human response to that divine grace, the issue is not whether to admit suitably qualified women to the presidency of the Eucharist, but whether the idea of an exclusive, qualified, authoritative cadre *at that place in Christian corporate life above all others* is not completely missing the point. Ought not *that* role to be open to all - the infirm, the uneducated, the failures, the children? After all, it calls for no talents! *Anyone could* do it. And if Christ is indeed in all of us equally, then anyone *should* do it. For preaching, counselling, healing, direction, administration, scholarship, art, music and many other things, gifts are required, and obviously *not* everyone should be entrusted with such things. But for so-called priestly functions, Eucharist, blessing, absolution, the efficacy is all of God, and that is best expressed by cutting human 'qualifications' (what could they be anyway?) to the minimum. The basic question is not the membership of the ministry, but, in this particular matter, the need for ministry at all.

Of course, once crack the traditional link between eucharistic presidency and qualification for other jobs in the Church, and everything is opened up. In such a situation we might see more clearly where the male–female issue comes into the matter. As many secular thinkers have seen, the real question is not whether women are to be allowed to play man-designed roles in a man-designed world, but whether women can be allowed to be themselves sufficiently to disagree and to change the man-designed world and the kind of roles people play within it. In the context of relations between the sexes, therefore, the question for the Church is: Are women to be allowed to influence the shaping of the Church of the future? What structures, what jobs really need there be? My guess is that this is the project for which the present is the *kairos*, God's right time. The danger, therefore, might be that a victorious campaign to admit women to the ministry we have got would both perpetuate what God wants to end and neutralize their capacity for the real changes that in the divine wisdom they are needed to make.

Having said that, however, I do not want to stop there. If we look yet more closely at the history of the people of God in the Bible and in the Church, we notice something else. That history, because it is God's history, is a purposeful line; but because it is human history as well, it is also a zig-zag one. (Indeed I am not sure that some of the zigs aren't so sharp they actually go backwards!) Take the Old Testament again, and read the debate about kingship in 1 Samuel. This might almost be called a paradigm case. Kingship is *the* thing in the world at large. 'Make us a king like all the nations.' In the controversy that followed two strongly opposed views emerge: one, that kingship means rebellion against Yahweh, an end to the true ethos of Israel's life as a free egalitarian community with all its members in a covenant relationship with Yahweh; the other, that God himself wills to raise up a hereditary monarchy to preserve his people in a hostile world. So ambivalent is the situation that both readings of the *kairos* are, in the narrative, put forcefully into the mouth of Samuel. In the end, as we know, kingship prevails; and very quickly (note this!) the supporters of the kingship assume that because it was God's will at that time, it is God's will for ever. The Davidic house may go through bad times, if it disobeys God, but it will never come to an end. This is the final form and structure for God's people. Of course, this was not so. The monarchy lasted just over four hundred years, and for one hundred and thirty-five years of that only over part of the nation. But the priestly law-based theocracy that eventually succeeded it also assumed that this time they had got it right for keeps. It's only natural, I suppose. God being absolute and eternal, if you feel you have rumbled his will at any given time, you feel it must be itself something permanent. That is our natural response to Godness. And let us be quite clear that the fact that any particular system doesn't go on for ever doesn't mean it wasn't God's will when it came in. 'God fulfils himself in many ways' – because he *does* take history seriously. He made it. The other point I want you to notice is that the whole time kingship was in operation it was subjected to constant critique and pressure. Its limitations as a means of response to the will of God became apparent very quickly; and all sorts of things were attempted to improve its performance in this respect.

The history of the Church is marked with similar institutional developments. The most striking parallel, I suppose, is the papacy. But the ordained ministry is certainly another. It evolved partly out of practical necessity, when Gentile Christians were scattered individuals, many of them slaves, and a family/house church pattern was difficult to sustain, and worship had to be at times when everyone could get away and gather at a special meeting-place from all over town. A new community system had to emerge, with officially appointed leaders to preside at the Eucharist, and exercise pastoral and business discipline. In time the various sketches of an ethos for this leadership converged on something that was a Christian version both of the Jewish priesthood and of pagan priest-hoods, with more than a touch of Roman civil structure thrown in. At the same time specifically Christian theology also played its part in reinterpreting these structures and giving the emergent pattern a Christian character. But it was continuous evolution. The developments of eucharistic theology, medieval responses to the changing relation of Church and State, and many other things played their part. For many Christians this tradition was radically revolutionized at the Reformation. The threefold apostolic ministry, the sacrificing priesthood, came to an end. New ways were found of fulfilling God's will at that *kairos*. Our preoccupation here is: Are we at another *kairos*? And if so, what does it demand of us?

Let me offer my own answer to those questions, which I hope is fairly straightforward and unequivocal. (i) Nothing we achieve in our generation will be the eternal answer, it will not even begin heading straight towards that answer, it will be zigging or zagging one way or another. (ii) We have to do what seems right to us, after thought and prayer, without worrying whether it seems right to God. If we do this we shall contribute something, however small, to the fulfilment of the total plan, which is hidden from us. (iii) What seems right to us may well derive from the non-ecclesiastical world around us. That is no disadvantage at all, because God is actually interested in that world; and also we need to remember that any course of action is right and rational, if it can be supported by impartial evidence and good moral and logical arguments, whatever its provenance. (iv) Some of the arguments deployed against the ordination of women, principally those concerned with the interpretation of Scripture, bring up fundamental issues relevant to all our discipleship, which the Church has not yet faced in its corporate decision-making. It is therefore vital to deal with these matters. We may not win the battle, but we must be rigorously honest in satisfying *ourselves* that at the intellectual level *we* have done all we can to discern the will of God here and now. (v) Finally, the really difficult question, if we say that there are new forms and expressions of priesthood to be discovered by all of us, and that women will have something fresh to bring to this, are we arguing for change in the priesthood so radical that many will feel it cannot be what God wills for his Church? Let me conclude by offering my own positive theological approach to this central question.

I believe that the threefold Catholic ministry has developed in the Church under the guidance of the Holy Spirit for a fundamental reason. In its three images of shepherd–guardian, priest and servant it expresses the three great saving activities of God in Christ: making known the truth and its meaning for life; offering oneself in prayer and love for others; serving human need. Christ himself did these things in his earthly ministry. The Church is called to do them now in ministering to the world.

What is more, this vocation is that of all Christ's followers. Different Christians have different gifts: teaching, healing, counselling, music, art, poetry, administration, speaking, leadership, and so forth. But *all*, to the limit of their opportunity, must proclaim the gospel, live lives of sacrificial prayer and love, care for others. In all Christ's members his Body is, as he was, shepherd, priest and servant to the world.

The ordained ministry is there as the structural means to ensure that the Church in each generation stays faithful to these primary roles, to form Christ in us individually and corporately so that we fulfil them better. It is for this purpose that authority to preach the Word and administer the sacramental means of grace is entrusted to them. Their job is to make us all shepherds, priests and servants.

I have to ask myself, therefore: if both men and women are meant by God to live out this episcopal, priestly and diaconal vocation to those around them, and have in fact been doing so for two thousand years, ought not both men and women also to be the spiritual enablers of this vocation? How indeed can the object be achieved otherwise? If the life of both sexes is to bear this essential character of shepherd, priest and servant, must not the ministry ordained to symbolize this life and develop it within the Church also be drawn from both sexes? Yes, it must. Women will bring new personal expressions to priesthood, to episcopacy; but it will still be priesthood, episcopacy they express. It is because of the essential character of Catholic order that I believe in ordination for women. It is because that character does not change that the 'right time' for such ordination is just as soon as our eyes have been opened to these hidden riches of our inheritance.

TWELVE

Snakes and Ladders:
Reflections on Hierarchy and the Fall

Peter Clark

In September of 1982, under the auspices of the Movement for the Ordination of Women, a group was set up in which 'feminist ideas could be looked at, explored, developed, particularly as far as they affect the Church and theology'.[1]* From its inception the MOW Theological Working Group, as it chose to call itself, was clear that not only should the *content* of its discussions and thinking be the relation of feminist insights to theology, but also that its *method* of working should embody, as far as possible, the conviction that it is vital to anchor thought in experience. Not exactly an original conviction, but the rediscovery of its importance is perhaps one of the more significant contributions of the feminist movement to contemporary thinking. At any rate we wanted to discover whether it was possible to find a new way of working.

Accordingly we appointed no chairwoman or chairman, and no permanent secretary, but took it in turns to supply these functions. We agreed that our chief aim was to reflect upon experience: our own as individuals, our own as a group, and that of other people. And out of this we would consider what our experience has to say to the traditions that we have inherited, and which have helped to form us. Tradition has a tendency to dictate the limits, or the validity, of experience, but we believe that this *double dynamic* - where each is formed, reappraised, renewed by the other - underlies the doing of all theology. In order to achieve anything of all this we determined to allow ourselves time. To resort to jargon, we committed

*The other members of the MOW Theological Working Group are Anthony Dyson, Ruth McCurry, Mick Moss, Christopher Rowland, Henriette Santer, Alma Servant and Mary Tanner.

ourselves to 'being' together and seeing what emerged, rather than 'doing' together in order to achieve some preordained goal. So far so good.

But no group exists in a vacuum, and after only a few meetings we began to experience a pressure to produce: the pressure of outside events, of our responsibility to MOW, and of our own internal needs to work for change and to respond to challenge. In this last category we all agreed that an article by the Bishop of London, eventually published in the *Epworth Review* of January 1984, was so totally unconvincing in its case against the ordination of women that it simply had to be answered. We therefore spent two sessions discussing the article and the drafts of our response, in which we were able to draw on the wide variety of expertise represented in our group. Almost immediately after completing this task, and before our reply had appeared in print (in *Theology*, March 1984), we became aware that the deadline for this present symposium was rapidly approaching. When the group first began to meet we had been told that SPCK might be interested in a contribution from us, and at that distance we had agreed to produce something. We did not realize, perhaps naively, that it takes a long time to establish new ways of working, or that a printer's deadline can be very inhibiting to freedom of exploration. And so, as we addressed ourselves to the task of drawing together the themes of our discussion for this essay, it became clear that we were in danger of becoming yet one more task-orientated committee, dedicated to the production of articles and reports – without giving ourselves time and space adequately to reflect, to deepen our insights, to overhaul (as one member of the group put it) our own views by listening to the experience of others. 'Looking for a lake to swim in,' said another, 'we found ourselves exposed on a mountain.'

Having allowed ourselves to be lured onto the mountainside, we agreed that we must accept the consequences, honour our commitments and produce the essay we had rashly promised. We agreed, however, that it was important that we should learn from this experience, and that in the future we should think very carefully indeed before yielding to any external (or internal) pressure towards the achievement of particular, short-term goals. We were also agreed that this pressure to achieve, to 'do', should inform at least some part of the content of this essay.

We bother to relate all this by way of introduction, partly because it provides the background for what follows, and partly because the group's experience is a paradigm of the dilemma facing those working for the ordination of women to the priesthood. In the urgency of the movement towards organizational reform (and we do not suggest that it is *not* urgent) there is a danger that we will lose sight of the wider implications for theology and for the Church in such a movement, that we will lose sight of what lies behind the impetus for change. If women priests are not simply to become absorbed, to acquiesce in the present rigid institutions of the established churches, if their distinctive contribution is not to be lost, then there needs to be a great deal of clear and painful heart-searching.

This process of reassessment began for us with a realization that behind all our individual experience, behind the experience of many others with whom we come into contact, was an aching sense of *disablement*: in many areas of life, but above all for us as Christians, a disablement in our understanding of, and experience of the totality of ministry. For ordained and unordained in parish life, in the synodical organization of the Church at all levels, in theological colleges, on church commissions, in our preaching and in our worship, in our approach to the sacramental, and also among those on the outside looking in, we experience frustration and disablement. In many cases it is the refusal of the Church to recognize the priestly ministry of women which has brought to the surface this awareness. But it has become obvious to us that it is something much deeper than that particular issue which is involved here. It is not a matter of anything so external as 'women's rights'; ultimately it is not even a matter of particular vocations. It is a matter of what the whole Church is called to be.

Rita Hannon, a La Sainte Union sister working in Tanzania, writing in *The Tablet*, said:

I need to have them [women] visibly present in religious services, at least sometimes, as those who exercise authority and minister. I have felt the need also of the feminine principle acknowledged in the language, images and symbols of worship. In admitting this, I am saying something about myself as female. I do not apologise when I assert: where my sister is not, I am not.[2]

We would want to point out that such a conviction is felt, even now, by men as well as by women. They too can say, 'Where my sister is not, I am not'. In claiming this we are saying something about ourselves as humans. Furthermore, in claiming this we are saying something also about our doctrine of God.

We believe that the question of the ordination of women, while important in itself, brings into focus these much broader questions – of our understanding of God and of humanity – and that it provides us with an opportunity, and a standpoint, from which to approach them. It is *not* a matter of tinkering with the details of organization. This sense of disablement of which we speak highlights a crisis at the deepest level in the life of the Church, a crisis moreover which is finding echoes in many other aspects of contemporary life. This is seen most vividly perhaps in the crisis brought about by the peace movement (in which women have played a central role); and in the crisis of Western capitalism, faced with its apparent failure to achieve any constructive solution to the problems of world poverty – or even to continue to sustain its own adherents. The fierceness of the reaction against the ordination of women within the establishment of the Church of England, the energy with which Western governments have attempted to counteract the impact of increased debate on the issues of nuclear arms, the intensification of the struggle between capitalism and Marxism (providing a smokescreen for failures on both sides) – all these point, in differing degrees, to the critical insecurity with which those in power regard the various challenges which confront their authority. For it is precisely the issue of power and authority which is at stake.

Women have for centuries been on the receiving end of the exercise of power and authority. They have been at the bottom, or at least at the very lowest levels, of a hierarchical pile, both within the churches and beyond. It is this cumulative experience which has taught women to question and to challenge not only their place within the hierarchies, but also the authenticity, the very validity of the hierarchies themselves. At first it appeared that women were claiming parity with men, and equal opportunities as regards positions of power. What now becomes clear is that it is not simply the male monopoly of power which is being challenged; it is nothing other than our understanding of the whole established order, and the exercise of power as such.

The grandiloquence of such a claim does not escape us. We had better try to defend it.

Hierarchy seems to have been, and seems to be, always and everywhere, a feature of the life of humankind in society. To live in community is to acknowledge the necessity of some degree of administrative organization – in order to ensure survival, to facilitate day-to-day existence, to provide the security within which alone growth is possible: physical, mental, emotional, moral and spiritual. The larger the community, the more elaborate the necessary structures become to maintain stability, continuity and identity. Yet in theory this necessity for organization does not automatically imply *hierarchy* – which for our present purposes we take to mean a 'sacred' order involving successive subordination. Of the many images used to describe the workings of the state, that of a body composed of mutually dependent members could be seen to be an argument *against* the concept of hierarchy. In St Paul's use of the image, for example,[3] it is the wholeness, the completeness of the body which is at stake. In this light a body without a foot is as incomplete, as disabled, as a body without a head. The ideal body is a non-hierarchical organism. In practice, however, experience shows that when we are not dealing in the realm of the ideal, a body can survive quite adequately without a foot, an arm or an eye. But it cannot survive without head, heart or lungs. And so *worth* and *function* become confused; distinctions of function become determinative of distinctions of worth. In our own group, faced with the pressure to produce written theological work as previously mentioned, we have had to guard against imposing feelings of inferiority on those members for whom the written, theological word is not a natural form of self-expression. In other words, how are we to affirm the distinctive value of each contribution to the group? This is something on which we continue to work; but our experience, even in this, points to the apparent ease, if not the inevitability, with which the organization necessary to achieve any set goal comes to be seen as hierarchical.

Perhaps this is to state the obvious. It is less easy to disentangle the religious dimension which appears to lie behind all this. The search for meaning in an apparently meaningless world, and the identification of that meaning with some notion of objectively defined divinity, transform utterly our apprehension of the structures of human society. No longer is the demarcation of function within society merely an administrative convenience; necessary structures become what we have claimed the word hierarchy implies – a *sacred* order. Function and worth are now indissolubly linked in a 'chain of being', and humanity with its minor pecking orders is seen as but one part of a much larger pecking order. For if authority, power, meaning, truth are all to be invested in the end term ('God') of an infinite sequence, how else are the worlds of the ultimate and of the provisional to be linked? How else is truth to be perceived in this shifting world of experience, if it is not handed down authoritatively from above? In this account, the security of all our human institutions depends – literally hangs from – the security of divine institutions, which by their very nature are understood to be static, unchanging, eternal. And it is God's supposed participation in this scheme which gives a sort of divine warranty or seal of approval for the maintenance of a successive subordination in the ordering of human society. In the Christian view, this appears to involve God as Father, Son and Holy Spirit devolving power within the Church to bishops, priests, deacons, the minor orders, lay men, and lay women; and in the secular state to emperors, kings, councillors, nobility, gentry, the professions, skilled and unskilled labour, and the unemployed.[4]

Now that is very crudely put; and of course enlightened twentieth-century minds do not picture a cosmic order of such laughable simplicity. There has been, after all, a Copernican revolution in our thought. Or has there? What of our behaviour

- our practice as opposed to our theory? If we look around at the static hierarchies of our institutions, both religious and secular, if we observe the zeal with which the *status quo* is defended, the almost universal reluctance to accept change - do we not begin to sense that behind all this, despite our protestations to the contrary, lies a profoundly dualistic view of cosmic order, from which we derive a comforting belief in the divine sanction of all our established institutions?

What we believe the women's movement is in fact saying to the hierarchies is: such a world view is no longer possible; the old images are dead; the symbols of authority and power which we used to justify our hierarchically ordered societies no longer work. It is as simple as that. It is as serious as that. Within the context of the Church this means that a hierarchical priesthood now has little or no relevance or significance - not only for women, but (in England at any rate) for all who are non-white, non-middle-class, non-literate, non-affluent, indeed for all who, by its exclusiveness, the Church treats as non-people. Because the priesthood as we know it today is too limited to be truly representative of society at large;[5] and because society is no longer prepared to collude in seeing the priesthood as representative in any worthwhile sense of God . . .

Of course, within the security of the institutions it is still possible to pretend that all is well. And precisely because it is their *power* that they are defending, the hierarchies of our institutions can exert considerable pressure to persuade us that nothing has really changed, that we can continue to go through the motions in confidence. But it is a thin kind of nourishment which they offer, and one which we can only accept with a bad conscience, as we huddle together for warmth and reassurance, turning our backs on those outside. We know in our hearts that the symbols no longer work. The wonder is that we managed to persuade ourselves for so long that they did.

As Christians this realization forces us to re-examine the content of the gospel and the figure at its heart. It forces us to re-examine our view of the human condition to which it claims to be an answer. It is surely no accident that the women's movement in the churches has coincided with the growth of the liberation theologies from the so-called Third World, as well as with the spread of the churches' involvement in the peace movement. For these are all radical movements in the strict sense of the word - seeking to tap the roots of the gospel message. And in so doing they have, in their different ways, highlighted that which should have been blindingly obvious, but which it has been easier to ignore: that the figure of Jesus is inescapably bound up with the concept of powerlessness. And conversely, the exercise of power and authority is inescapably bound up with *fallenness*.

According to the Genesis narrative,[6] it is the thirst for an illusory independence that brings about humanity's downfall. We long to be as God, with the power to decide, to 'know', for ourselves, not realizing that is only against God that we can *know* good and evil. The earliest consequence of the fall is an immediate denial of all sense of responsibility for our actions: 'The woman tempted me and I ate,' says the man; 'The serpent tempted me and I ate,' says the woman. The buck begins to pass . . . but already we see that here we are confronted by two of the chief characteristics of hierarchy: the need for, and exercise of, power; and the avoidance of responsibility. For before the Fall, God and his creation are at one, a harmonious network of interdependent beings in which mankind talks directly with God, and has no fear or shame before him. The serpent, however, presents a very different interpretation of reality - and introduces the possibility of hierarchy. For God, he says, is jealous to preserve his power and authority: 'God knows . . . that you will become like him.' And now God and creation are seen in a very different light. The wedge of dualism is driven home, and fear and shame become the keynotes. Banished from the garden, we no longer walk with God in the cool of the evening. He has become an annihilating threat. We can no longer talk *to* God, we can only talk *about* him (after all, the whole process began with the question, 'Did God say. . . ?') And now not only are we alienated from God, we are alienated from each other in relationships based on power, where the man against his will is the woman's master, and where she against her will 'burns for' her husband. Alienated too from the rest of creation (represented by the snake, and by the earth which now will only yield its fruit unwillingly), we are even alienated from ourselves. Man has become 'like God': 'He is the lord of this world, but now of course the solitary lord and despot of the mute, violated, silenced, dead world of his own ego.'[7] We may forge the concept of an elaborate chain of being to make sense of this alienation, but we cannot hide from ourselves that, in our loneliness and futility, we believe our lives to be preserved only for nothingness – 'Dust you are . . .' We cannot hide from ourselves our fear that the one vital link in the chain is missing, that God has cast us off utterly. The symbolism of hierarchy is self-imposed – and flawed.

If Christ is the second Adam, rescuing us from our fallen condition, then on this account we might expect his coming to effect an exposure of the godlessness of hierarchy, of the illusory nature of the game we are playing and of the barriers we erect. We might expect his message to centre on the abrogation of power, the acceptance of responsibility, the overcoming of fear, the restoration of self-esteem, the renewal of relationship within the human family and between it and God. And that is exactly what we do find. In the birth narratives, in the ministry and teaching, in the passion, crucifixion and resurrection of Jesus, the message is consistently one of God's being more at home with the poor and outcast, the dispossessed, the powerless; of a God who breaks down barriers (or reveals their unreality) and who puts down the mighty from their thrones. There is nothing new in this 'discovery'. Sadly, neither is there anything new in our ability to ignore it, to rationalize it away, to refuse to take it seriously. Nor should we be surprised; disciples have consistently misunderstood the significance of the gospel – 'Lord, who will be greatest in the kingdom of heaven?' – but it is disappointing that we consistently fail to learn from past mistakes. In the New Testament we see the foundations of a rigid hierarchism being dug from the earliest days of the Church. With the Lucan notion of ascension and heavenly session Jesus himself is transformed into a conventional authority figure. In the longing of the early epistles for a *second* coming 'in power' we detect more than a trace of dissatisfaction with the first coming, a reluctance to believe that God can finally be manifest in powerlessness. In a growing authoritarianism in the church; in its assimilation by the secular state after Constantine; in its encounter with neo-Platonism and in its working out of Trinitarian doctrine – in all of these we can trace the difficulty with which the early disciples worked out the implications of the gospel. Nor is it any easier for us.

In all of this we are not attempting to prove anything – hence the extreme brevity of this exposition of biblical and doctrinal themes. We are saying simply that we believe the witness of biblical insight bears out the truth which women and men have discovered, and are discovering in many areas of their lives, in many fields of experience: that hierarchy can no longer be regarded as a *God-given* pattern of human organization.[8] For hierarchy, as we have seen, is deeply bound up with fallenness – it is a fallen interpretation of the nature of reality. And as in the myth of the fall the need to pin the blame beyond ourselves gives rise to a belief in self-existent evil, and ultimately to a personalized 'devil', so with our experience of hierarchies do they come to have an apparently demonic vital force of their own, to which we rapidly become subject: 'I deeply regret this, but the demands of the system require . . . that you be unemployed, that you be refused ordination, that you must subscribe to the theory of nuclear deterrence, that your child must starve . . .' Reliance on hierarchy is in a sense the very antithesis of incarnation. For how can God possibly be 'with us' when by our doctrine and by our administrative structures, by our architecture and by our worship, by the poverty of our spirituality we proclaim that we believe him to be not Emmanuel, but a discarnate Absolute Authority, and Minister of Just Deserts?

The foregoing might seem to lead to the conclusion that the only way forward would be to jettison completely the concept of hierarchy – both from our theology and from the way in which we organize society. By the same token, it might appear that we have also to abandon every notion of the transcendence of God. But the implication here is not a shallow utopianism,[9] any more than we are claiming that God is only to be seen as immanent. It is often assumed that the only alternative to hierarchy is anarchy (anarchy and utopianism being, for our purposes, but two sides of the same coin). But there is another possibility.

The transcendence of God has to be discovered in, with and through our experience of the immanence of God – if we are to be true at all to the whole notion of incarnation and not fall over into the dualism and docetism[10] which, to be frank, has distorted so much Christian thought over nearly twenty centuries. Similarly, our discovery of the powerlessness of authentic humanity, of divine strength made perfect in human weakness – and hence of the inadequacy of hierarchy as a model on which to base our lives – this discovery can only be made in, with and through the present structures of power and authority. The paradox here is that it is immanence and power, transcendence and powerlessness which seem to belong together in pairs, rather than the other way around, as might conventionally be expected. For if immanence is God subject to the world of fallen humanity, this present world of the exercise of power and authority, then transcendence is God glimpsed in a world of redeemed and redeeming humanity, a world of the abrogation of power and authority. These seeming opposites are reconciled in the person of Jesus, and above all on the cross, which says, amongst so much else, that we cannot turn our backs upon the fact that this is a fallen world, or free ourselves from the limitations which it imposes – above all from suffering and death. But at the same time neither can we accept our fallen condition as fixed and final. Suffering and death are not the whole truth.

So what all this means, what we have been a long time driving at, is the necessity of seeing all our hierarchies not as *God-given* (at least, precisely not as God-given if by that we mean 'God-approved', 'God-willed') but as *provisional*. Furthermore we must learn to see them as the place in which we are to strive towards the possibility of a non-hierarchical understanding of our world. There *is* then a sense in which the hierarchies are given to us by God, just as the fallen world is given to us: they are given to be transformed, to be the focus of our 'divine discontent'. If the world is the place where we are to work out our salvation, then our hierarchical institutions are the place where we must work out our liberation from authoritarianism.

Openness, adaptability, might be said to be the key-notes of the shift away from a hierarchical understanding of the nature of society. The ability to listen, to hold a silence, to meet people where they are, to admit that one may be mistaken, to receive forgiveness when it is offered as well as to offer it where it is needed - these would be some of the characteristics of a life redeemed from hierarchy. Yet how many of our church institutions at parochial, deanery, diocesan or national levels have begun to reflect anything of all this? At a recent spiritual direction course (where, if anywhere, one might have hoped to encounter a more conscious degree of sensitivity) during one of the 'de-briefing' sessions, seven able and experienced women ministers sat silent while the fourteen priests participating in the course competed to talk of their reactions to the session under review . . . Again, two deaconesses known to the group told of separate instances where they had preached on the theme of God's power made perfect in weakness, only to be immediately followed by intercessions, led by priests, which concentrated on the might and majesty of God. In neither case did these deaconesses consider that the prayers had been offered as an inapposite rebuke to their preaching. It appeared to be simply an inability on the part of those priests (and perhaps many others) to hear what they were trying to say, to be open to other than conventional ways of thinking about God.

It is everyday experiences like these (and parallels are not hard to come by, outside the sphere of ministry) which confirm the crushing sense of disablement women feel today at the apparent non-relevance of their thinking. It is experiences like these which confirm the conviction in us that women are drawing attention to areas of thinking and feeling without which our understanding of God and of humanity must be incomplete. It is perhaps above all the *superficiality* of the Church's own self-understanding, and the *superficiality* of what it is saying about the God it claims to represent, that is the most disheartening aspect of the current situation. The Church is quite simply failing to meet the deepest needs of too many women and men.

Perhaps, then, it will be necessary to try to find a new word to describe our institutions. For 'hierarchy' - *sacred* order -

resonates too strongly with the ideas associated with a dualistic, 'God-willed', chain-of-being view of the world. It suggests a self-satisfied status quo. But new words, convincing words, are not easily found. Perhaps they will emerge. But first of all we need to recognize that all our institutions (Sabbath, government, marriage, local councils, priesthood . . .) are made for us, not we for them – and made for us as the framework within which we are called to rediscover the divine image in one another, and within ourselves. When they cease to achieve this, when ways are perceived in which they could more fully achieve this, then the institutions must be ready, indeed anxious, to change.

Change will inevitably involve tension, between that which has been and that which is coming into being; and tension leads to conflict. The Church (quite unjustifiably in view of its origins) has always been particularly shy of conflict. But this is largely because it has failed to distinguish between conflict and violence. Hence its deep suspicion of all change. For if change leads to tension, and tension leads to conflict, what is to prevent conflict spilling over into violence? Better, therefore, to avoid the risk – better no change. Particularly when the Church can appeal to the age-old bogey of schism, *and* to a fixed and immutable cosmic order as justification for a fixed and immutable earthly order. It is true of course that the readiness to face up to conflict can provoke violence in others – the women of Greenham know this today; Gandhi knew it; as Christians we need look no further than the cross to see that this is so. But where the violent exercise of power is not colluded with, where violence is not returned for violence – then the power of 'power' is broken, or revealed to be a sham. And that is when new possibilities are revealed. We cannot escape it: change, and the readiness to be changed are at the heart of the gospel. This applies to institutions and communities every bit as much as to individuals. That change is possible *is* the Good News.

The implications of all this for the ordination of women to the priesthood will be obvious. Those who oppose such a move cannot, for one moment, claim that they are fighting for a better and more inclusive framework in which more women and men can discover their full potential as children of God. Put like that, it is clear that theirs is a rearguard action, seeking simply to defend a narrow power-base, which works only for an increasingly limited cross-section of humanity. They leave too many people out. We will never solve the problems of 'lay ministry' until we have grappled with the message of feminist thought for theology, and until we have learned to see the priesthood in genuinely representative and inclusive, rather than exclusive, terms. For, as long as the priesthood is understood as being bound up with the exercise of power and authority, we can only go on inviting lay ministers (what does the title really mean?) to become honorary climbers of our hierarchies; and any real sense of 'the priesthood of all believers' will remain an impossibility, on the Gilbertian grounds that 'if everyone is somebody, then no one's anybody'. But as previously stated, the implications range much wider than issues of church order, and must be seen to be wider. Indeed, one of the difficulties in writing this article has been to convey, on very small canvas, something of the immensity of the change in our thinking which is needed *and which is already coming about.*

So, organization and institutions are necessary in the ordering of a fallen world; but we must learn to see them as provisional, not as corresponding to some divine and immutable blueprint. But if it is going to be difficult to find a word to replace 'hierarchy' it is going to be no less difficult to find new images and symbols to sustain and nourish us. If we can no longer see the universe in terms of a great pyramid, or chain, of being, what pictures are we going to use to describe it? Symbols, like words, emerge rather than being coined or chosen. Carol Gilligan has suggested that

> The reinterpretation of women's experience in terms of their own imagery of relationships . . . clarifies that experience and also provides a non-hierarchical vision of human connection. Since relationships when cast in the imagery of hierarchy appear inherently unstable and morally problematic, their transposition with the image of *web* changes an order of inequality into a structure of inter-connection.[11]

But the 'web' image is perhaps no less problematic. If God is not to be found at the apex of a pyramid, neither is God to be found at the centre of a web. The fear of being trapped by a divine spider (always female!) is as offensive to male sensibilities as the fear of being oppressed by a divine despot (always male!) is to female sensibilities. We need an image of relatedness which will be characterized by openness, supportiveness, inclusiveness and mutuality. Perhaps the image of one body made up of many parts is still the most easily accessible, providing always that it is the *wholeness* of the body which is emphasized. Perhaps instead we need the model of some infinite, three dimensional network (such as the universe itself?) with God in every particle and as the sum total of an infinity of particles. But that would be to move away from the realm of symbolism towards that of scientific description.

Whatever the image will be, it will be at once both simple and profound. The only symbolism which has never entirely failed within the Christian context - and it has parallels in many other cultures - is the Eucharist. In spite of all attempts by a male priesthood to make it the last bastion of all ecclesiastical hierarchy, authority and power ('You cannot reach up to God, nor he down to you, without my priestly mediation'), the sacramental giving and receiving of bread and wine has never ceased to be a symbol of relatedness, and of transcendence *through* immanence. Nor has it ever totally lost its power to move, and to include all sorts and conditions of God's people - even where it has been deliberately misused as a principle of exclusion or as a means of control. It has provided, and it still provides, a context within which we can discover our common humanity, can rediscover the lost image of God in one another and in ourselves. If we could learn to see the President at the Eucharist not as a divinely validated authority figure, but as the accepted representative and servant of the gathered congregation, then we might begin to appreciate just what it is we say when 'We break this bread to share in the Body of Christ'. But the priesthood of all believers cannot be anything more than a pious shibboleth while women are refused ordination. Until our ideas of priesthood have been renewed by the insights of contemporary experience, including that of women, the Eucharist will not be set free to become what it already is: the place where we meet together at our most human; the place where we come together to demonstrate our *need* - of food and drink, of one another, and of God - and our *responsibility* - for one another, and to God. It can be no accident that the first words of the Beatitudes are, 'How blest are those who know their need . . .' For need, and its corollary, responsibility, in the Christian vision, are the fundamental truths of the human condition. Those who know themselves to be dispossessed, to be in need, for whatever reason, transcend the limitations of fallenness and do not use hierarchy as a means of hiding from God, of keeping God at a safe distance.

The symbolism is all still there, waiting to be set free. It is the primary gospel imagery of human need and of divine grace. We must re-establish its content for the poor and outcast of today's world - ourselves among them - by stripping away the secondary (and second-rate) accretions of much ecclesiastical and hierarchical symbolism. For it is only by listening to the powerless, by learning from their experience, that the Church will be able to turn from a dead authoritarianism to the real authority and power with which Jesus spoke, and which so astonished those who heard him - the authority and power of truth.

This essay has touched upon a wide variety of themes - many of them of great complexity and depth. It is presented simply as 'work in progress', or as a *report* of work in progress. The 'finished' article will not be a more comprehensive or coherent essay or book. It will be the sharing and deepening of insights, first of all within the MOW Theological Working Group as it continues to explore these themes, but also amongst any who may be stimulated or provoked into dialogue by what they read here. Finally, the 'finished article' will be the living out of our insights, as we commit ourselves to the transforming of our parishes and homes, our work or worklessness, the groups we belong to, our relationships or our isolation - every aspect of life - into places where we and others may begin to discover the presence of God: with us all, in our need.

Notes

1. From a paper by Monica Furlong for the Central Council of MOW, 28 November 1981.
2. 'A Nun's Complaint', *The Tablet*, 26 November 1983, pp. 1151-2.
3. e.g. 1 Corinthians 12.12-31.
4. Of course, this view is greatly over simplified, and the traffic is not all in one direction. Our experience of human hierarchies obviously affects the way we picture the 'higher' hierarchies. But the principal movement is a downwards one. Does the liberation theologian's call to 'do theology from below' go far enough if it simply seeks to change the direction, rather than challenging the whole notion of hierarchy as 'given'?
5. It may be asked whether the priesthood was ever truly representative of society in any age. But as long as the concept of a chain, or pyramid of being, underpinned the fabric of society, it was not the *representative* nature of the priesthood that was all important. It was rather the almost mechanical idea that one higher up the ladder was prepared to mediate with God on behalf of those on the lower rungs.
6. Genesis 3 - a passage which well repays detailed study.
7. Dietrich Bonhoeffer, *Creation and Fall* (SCM, 1959), p. 92.
8. Jesus' own choice of the Twelve and later of the seventy-two, often regarded as central to the so-called case against women's ordination, need not be seen as divine endorsement of hierarchical structures. It simply means that Jesus was a man of his time, subject to the practical limitations of life in a fallen world. And the commission to spread the Good News was not a call to honour and power; quite the reverse, it was a call to suffering.
9. 'Utopianism' does not here refer to any of the classic presentations of such a concept - Plato, Moore *et al*. Interestingly enough, their utopian systems are characterized by extreme forms of hierarchy. We use the term to suggest (or rather to refute!) the idea that all structures and organization can be dispensed with, any more than we can simply 'dispense' with the fact of our fallenness.
10. *Dualism* is a style of thinking rather than a distinct system. Generally it denotes a conviction that reality is comprised of two irreducibly different constituents - spirit and matter. One result of such a division was, and is, *docetism* (again, a tendency rather than a coherent doctrine) which sees the humanity of Christ as apparent rather than real; a sort of edifying divine charade.
11. Carol Gilligan, *In a Different Voice* (Harvard University Press, 1982), p. 62 (our italics).